Campbell Curriculum

Orton-Gillingham Word List Dictionary

Volume 1:
Consonants,
Short Vowels, FLOSS,
Blends, End Blends,
Compound Words,
Closed Syllable Exceptions

by Valerie Arredondo, M.A.T.

Orton-Gillingham Word List Dictionary Series

Volume 1	**Volume 2**	**Volume 3**
Consonants Short Vowels FLOSS Blends End Blends Compound Words Closed Syllable Exceptions	Digraphs & Trigraphs VCE (silent E) Vowel Teams Sounds of Y Compound Words	R-Controlled W-Combinations Soft C & G -CLE (Stable Syllables) Silent Letter teams Complex Letter Teams -ED, -ES, -EST

Future Volumes

Volume 4	**Volume 5**
Syllable Types Syllable Division Multi-Syllable Words Compound Types Contractions	Prefixes Suffixes Schwa Roman roots Greek roots Multi-Syllable Words

Table of Contents

Table of Contents

Table of Contents

Table of Contents

Ideas for Using this Book

- ❖ The lists in this series are designed to be used by any Orton-Gillingham based instructor or teacher. It does not matter what order or program you are using.

- ❖ Design your lessons easily by looking up any letter or letter team. The **Table of Contents** makes it easy find whatever you need.

- ❖ The **LT's** column is a list of all the additional letters and letter teams in the word. (In this book phonograms are referred to as letters or letter teams).

- ❖ The **LT's** column can to help you choose fair words. In the list below (for the blend **BL**), you can see that the word **blab** has no other letter teams, besides **BL**. The word **black** has **-ck**, the word blade has **a-e**, and the word Blair has **ai**. This makes it easy to look at the list and quickly choose the words that would be fair words for your student.

Base	LT's	-s/-es	-ed	-ing	-y/-ly	-er	-est
blab		blabs	blabbed	blabbing		blabber	
black	-ck	blacks	blacked			blacker	blackest
blade	a-e	blades					
Blair	ai						
Blake	a-e						
blame	a-e	blames	blamed	blaming		blamer	

- ❖ Use the Letter Team column to find words that reinforce recently learned concepts. In the list below **(-NK),** if your student needed more practice with **R-blends**, you could look in the Letter Team column to find **-NK** words that also have **R-Blends**. **(brink, drink)**

Base	LT's	-s/-es	-ed	-ing	-y/-ly	-er	-est
blink	bl	blinks	blinked	blinking		blinker	
brink	br						
chink	ch	chinks	chinked	chinking			
clink	cl	clinks	clinked	clinking			
drink	dr	drinks		drinking		drinker	
ink		inks	inked	inking			

❖ Keep this book handy during lessons, in case your student needs extra practice with a specific phonogram.

❖ Use the details and rules listed under each phonogram to fully understand how that phonogram is used in the English language. Below is an example of a detail in the **FLOSS** section:

- **SS** follows the **FLOSS** rule. **F, L, S**, and **Z** are usually doubled at the end of a one-syllable short-vowel word. There are some exceptions to this rule.
- The double **SS** indicates that the word ending in **S** is not plural.
- Words that end in **SS** indicate a plural by adding **-ES**, instead of **-S** (**bless - blesses**).

❖ Use the word lists and letter teams columns to make review lesson for students. If you are using a structured curriculum, sometimes the curriculum will proceed too quickly for some students. These lists make it easy to create review lessons.

❖ Use the phonogram columns for each word to eliminate words that have letter teams your students have not learned yet.

❖ Design matrixes with inflectional endings. See the Resources section for matrixes and many other templates you can use with your students.

❖ Practice reading and spelling words with suffixes. Each list includes a column for the suffixes **-s, -es, 's, -ed, -ing, -y, -ly, -er/-ar/-or** and **-est**. For names that have apostrophe 'S for a name, the apostrophe 'S indicates possession and not the plural form of a word.

Base	-s/-es/'s	-ed	-ing	-y/-ly	-er/-ar/-or	-est
fun				funny	*funnier*	*funniest*
gum	gums	gummed	gumming	gummy	*gummier*	*gummiest*

❖ Print out individual phonogram cards for each student you are teaching. You can print the cards on paper, or card stock. Cards can be laminated, as well.

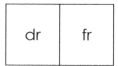

❖ Give your students their own phonogram cards so they can draw key word pictures on the cards. Send an extra set of cards home for extra practice.

❖ Make sorting lists, based on different phonograms. (See the Resources section for Word Frame templates and Sorting Cards templates).

❖ Help your students make word sums with the Word Sums template.

play + ing = playing

❖ Print the Letter and Phonogram Tiles (from the Resource section) onto paper or tagboard to make affordable manipulatives for Word Building activities.

| st | ing |

| b | a | t |

❖ Make games with the Bingo boards and Blank Card templates. You can also use the blank phonogram cards and spelling tiles cards to make games.

❖ Use the Resources List to find books that are informative about dyslexia, phonics, and word study.

❖ Use the Glossary to understand confusing terms.

Example #1

There are numerous ways to use this book. Here is an example of OG practitioner, Cindy. Cindy is tutoring a single student.
Cindy is introducing the FLOSS rule today and starting with the phonogram **-SS**. Below is (part of) the **FLOSS** rule list for the phonogram **-SS**.

Base	LT's	-s/-es	-ed	-ing	-y/-ly	-er	-est
bass							
Bess							
bless	bl	blesses	blessed	blessing			
bliss	bl						
boss		bosses	bossed	bossing	bossy		
chess	ch						

Cindy wants to make a reading practice list. She has taught her student blends, but has not yet taught digraphs. As an instructor, she can choose the words **bass**, **Bess** and **boss** immediately because she sees from the **LT's** column that those words do not contain any additional letter teams. She can also choose the words **bless** and **bliss**, because she has taught the **BL** blend previously. However, Cindy will leave the word **chess** off her list, because she has not taught the digraph **CH** before.

Cindy photocopies a reading list page from the resources section of this book.

She makes the following reading list for her students to read:

bass

Bess

boss

bless

bliss

Cindy makes an additional list of **SS** words for her students to practice spelling. The **SS** list is extensive, so Cindy knows if her students have trouble or need review, she can find more **SS** words for additional practice.

The next day, Cindy wants to challenge her students. She chooses compound words from the **SS** compound list that are fair words for her students.

sundress   crabgrass

Example #2

Here is an example for **OG** practitioner, Dave, who is tutoring a small group:

Dave has recently taught the **SS (FLOSS)** phonogram, and he would like his students to review **SS**. Dave's students have learned both blends and digraphs, so Dave can choose any word on the list.

Base	LT's	-s/-es	-ed	-ing	-y/-ly	-er	-est
bless	bl	blesses	blessed	blessing			
bliss	bl						
boss		bosses	bossed	bossing	bossy		
chess	ch						
class	cl	classes			classy		
cross	cr	crosses	crossed	crossing	crossly	crosser	
dress	dr	dresses	dressed	dressing	dressy	dresser	

Dave wants his students to practice adding the **-ES** at the end of a word to make it plural. Dave chooses the words in the list that have an **-ES** suffix on them. He does not choose the words **bliss** or **chess**, because those two words do not have an inflectional form that adds **-ES**.

Dave copies the word sum page in the back of the book, and has his students practice word sums with the words he has chosen from the list:

bless + es = blesses

boss + es = bosses

class + es = classes

cross + es = crosses

dress + es = dresses

Example #3

Karen is a student doing her first practicum. She is in a specific program that tells her the exact words and sentences she needs to use every day. However, Karen's practicum student is having trouble with the short /a/ sound. The program that Karen is using moves too fast for this student.

Karen needs to do a review of the short A sound, and because of that, she needs to come up with new words that have the short A that are not in her program's curriculum. Karen looks at the short A list and finds 5 new words that were not included in her program that all have a short A in them.

Base	-s/-es	-ed	-ing	-y/-ly	-er	-est
bad				badly		
bag	bags	bagged	bagging		bagger	
ban	bans	banned	banning		banner	
bat	bats	batted	batting	batty	batter	
cab	cabs			cabby		
Cam						
can	cans	canned	canning		canner	
cap	caps	capped	capping			

Karen chooses bad, bag, cab, and can. She copies the blending drill page from the resources section at the back of the book, and she uses those words as a blending drill for her student:

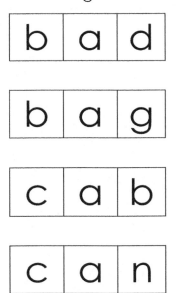

6

Example #4

Gary teaches structured literacy to a large class. Some of his students are high-level readers and some are struggling readers. Gary wants to have his class work on practice doubling a consonant before adding a vowel suffix.

Gary plans to have most of the class work on this concept individually, and he plans to pull out his group of struggling readers for extra help. Gary uses the same short A list that Karen used above:

Base	-s/-es	-ed	-ing	-y/-ly	-er	-est
bad				badly		
bag	bags	bagged	bagging		bagger	
ban	bans	banned	banning		banner	
bat	bats	batted	batting	batty	batter	
cab	cabs			cabby		
Cam						
can	cans	canned	canning		canner	
cap	caps	capped	capping			

Gary chooses words from the **-ED** and **-ING** columns that have a doubled consonant before adding **-ED** and **-ING**. Gary chooses the matrix resource page from the resources section at the end of this volume. He makes a photocopy of the matrix page, then he adds the base words and suffixes that he wants his students to practice.

Gary has the high-level readers in his class work on this page individually, while he pulls out his smaller group of struggling readers and helps them to do the matrix page together.

Root	Suffix
bag	-s
bat	-ed
	-ing

bags _____   bats _____

bagged _____   batted _____

bagging _____   batting _____

7

Helpful Tips

- Spellings and sounds of words and letter teams are in **bold** print. Sounds are indicated by slash marks /**sh**/ in **ship.**

- Compound words are listed immediately after each letter teams' list.

- The **LT's** column is a list of all the additional Letter Teams (phonograms) that are included in a word.

- Volumes 1-3 in this series are designed to be one-syllable and compound words. Future volumes will cover multi-syllable words. Multi-syllable words are provided in this volume only if the number of single-syllable words is limited. Multi-syllable words are likely to have schwa sounds, which may be difficult for students to spell.

- The single letter/short vowel word lists (ABC's) do not include any additional Letter Teams (blends, digraphs, etc.), since letter teams are always taught after single-letter words.

- Interesting facts and spelling rules related to each letter team are provided at the top of each word list. Students should not be expected to memorize all the details and rules that apply to each letter team. Those details and rules are provided for the teacher to fully understand the letter team and its usage. Students will learn the necessary rules and details over time.

- Words listed with italics in the base word column and a * in the **LT's** column indicate an unusual or unexpected spelling. The letter team that is marked with the star is irregular.

- Words listed in the **-er** and **-est** columns that are in italics are words that were formed from the **-y** form of the word (hair/hairy/hairier/hairiest). They were not formed from the base word that is listed at the beginning of the row. Some words in the base words column already have affixes attached to them, and therefore many of these words are not pure roots. That is why they are referred to as base words and not root words.

- Names in this book include their apostrophe form and not their plural form. Please note that apostrophe **'S** is not the plural of a name. It indicates possession. The word "Pat's" mean's something belongs to Pat. The word "Pats" indicates that there are more than one Pat.

Vowels – Printable Cards

a	e
i	o

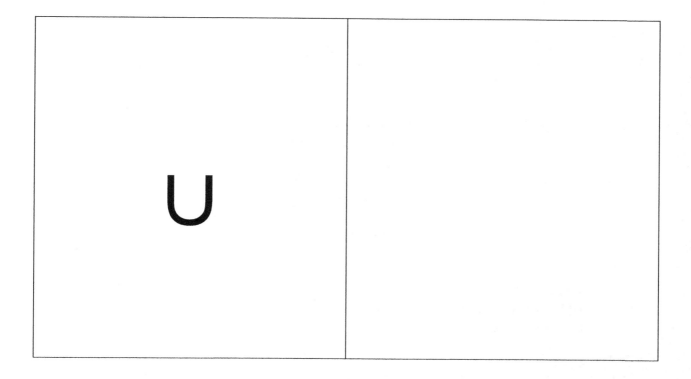

a

/ă/ in ax

Position: Beginning & Middle

Vocalization: Voiced

Classification: Short Vowel

- **A** is the second most common vowel, following **E**.
- **AM** and **AN** have a more nasal quality, and therefore they may be confusing for some students.

Beginning

	Base	-s/-es	-ed	-ing	-y/-ly	-er	-est
ad		ads					
am							
an							
as							
at							
ax		axes	axed	axing			

Middle

	Base	-s/-es/'s	-ed	-ing	-y/-ly	-er	-est
bad					badly		
bag		bags	bagged	bagging		bagger	
ban		bans	banned	banning		banner	
bat		bats	batted	batting	batty	batter	
cab		cabs			cabby		
Cam		Cam's					
can		cans	canned	canning		canner	
cap		caps	capped	capping			
dab		dabs	dabbed	dabbing		dabber	
dad		dads					
Dad		Dad's			Daddy		

Base	-s/-es/'s	-ed	-ing	-y/-ly	-er	-est
dam	dams	dammed	damming			
fad	fads					
fan	fans	fanned	fanning			
fat	fats			fatty	fatter	fattest
gab	gabs	gabbed	gabbing	gabby	gabber	
gag	gags	gagged	gagging			
gal	gals					
gap	gaps					
gas	gasses			gassy	*gassier*	*gassiest*
had						
ham	hams	hammed	hamming		hammer	
has						
hat	hats					
jab	jabs	jabbed	jabbing		jabber	
jam	jams	jammed	jamming		jammer	
lab	labs					
lad	lads					
lag	lags	lagged	lagging			
lap	laps	lapped	lapping			
lax				laxly		
Mac	Mac's					
mad				madly	madder	maddest
man	man's			manly	manner	
map	maps	mapped	mapping		mapper	
Max	Max's					
nab	nabs	nabbed	nabbing			
nag	nags	nagged	nagging		nagger	
Nan	Nan's					
nap	naps	napped	napping		napper	
pad	pads	padded	padding			
pal	pals					
pan	pans	panned	panning			
pat	pats	patted	patting		patter	
Pat	Pat's					
rag	rags	ragged				
ram	rams	rammed	ramming		rammer	
ran						
rap	raps	rapped	rapping		rapper	
rat	rats	ratted	ratting			
sag	sags	sagged	sagging			
sap	saps	sapped	sapping			
sat						

Base	-s/-es	-ed	-ing	-y/-ly	-er	-est
tab	tabs	tabbed	tabbing			
tag	tags	tagged	tagging		tagger	
tan	tans	tanned	tanning		Tanner	
tap	taps	tapped	tapping		tapper	
tax	taxes	taxed	taxing			
vac	vacs					
van	vans					
vat	vats					
wag	wags	wagged	wagging			
wax	waxes	waxed	waxing			
yak	yaks					
yam	yams				yammer	
yap	yaps	yapped	yapping		yapper	
zap	zaps	zapped	zapping		zapper	

e

/ĕ/ in jet

Position: Middle

Vocalization: Voiced

Classification: Short Vowel

- **E** is the most common letter in the alphabet.
- The letter **E** has many different functions. See the chart, *Jobs of the Letter **E*** in Volume 2 for more information on the letter **E**.

Middle

Base	-s/-es/'s	-ed	-ing	-y/-ly	-er/-ar	-est
bed	beds	bedded	bedding			
beg	begs	begged	begging		beggar	
bet	bets	betted	betting		better	
Deb	Deb's					
den	dens					
fed						
get	gets		getting		getter	
hem	hems	hemmed	hemming			
hen	hens					
hex	hexes	hexed	hexing			
jet	jets	jetted	jetting			
Ken	Ken's					
led						
leg	legs	legged	legging			
let	lets		letting		letter	
men	men's					
met						
net	nets	netted	netting			
peg	pegs	pegged	pegging			
Peg	Peg's		Peggy			

e

Base	-s/-es	-ed	-ing	-y/-ly	-er	-est
pen	pens	penned	penning	penny		
pep				peppy	pepper	
pet	pets	petted	petting			
red						
ref	refs					
rep	reps					
set	sets		setting		setter	
Ted	Ted's					
ten	tens					
vet	vets	vetted	vetting			
vex	vexes	vexed	vexing			
web	webs	webbed	webbing			
wet				wetly	wetter	wettest
yen	yens					
yes	yesses					
yet						

i̲

/ĭ/ in big

Position: Beginning and Middle

Vocalization: Voiced

Classification: Short Vowel

- Words of English origin do not end in the letter **i**. The words that do end in **i** are borrowed from other world languages (**ski, chili**), and from the Latin plural (**fungus – fungi**).
- The capital **I (i)** is often confused with the lowercase **L (l)**, because in many fonts, they look identical. Capital **I** traditionally had a top and bottom line **I** that made it more distinguishable from lowercase **L**

Beginning

Base	-s/-es	-ed	-ing	-y/-ly	-er	-est
if						
in						
is						
it						

Middle

Base	-s/-es	-ed	-ing	-y/-ly	-er	-est
bib	bibs					
bid	bids		bidding		bidder	
big						bigger	biggest
bin	bins	binned	binning			
bit						bitter	
did						
dig	digs		digging		digger	
dim	dims	dimmed	dimming	dimly	dimmer	dimmest
din						dinner	

Base	-s/-es	-ed	-ing	-y/-ly	-er	-est
dip	dips	dipped	dipping		dipper	
fib	fibs	fibbed	fibbing		fibber	
fig	figs					
fin	fins	finned	finning			
fix	fixes	fixed	fixing		fixer	
gig	gigs					
hid						
him						
hip	hips					
his						
hit	hits		hitting		hitter	
jib	jibs					
jig	jigs					
kid	kids	kidded	kidding		kidder	
kin						
Kip	Kip's					
Kit	Kit's					
lid	lids	lidded				
lip	lips					
lit						
mix	mixes	mixed	mixing		mixer	
nib	nibs					
nil						
nip	nips	nipped	nipping	nippy	nipper	
nix	nixes	nixed	nixing			
pic	pics					
pig	pigs	pigged	pigging	piggy		
pin	pins	pinned	pinning		pinner	
pip	pips					
pit	pits	pitted	pitting			
rib	ribs	ribbed	ribbing			
rid						
rig	rigs	rigged	rigging			
rim	rims	rimmed				
rip	rips	ripped	ripping		ripper	
sin	sins	sinned	sinning		sinner	
sip	sips	sipped	sipping			
sit	sits		sitting		sitter	

Base	-s/-es	-ed	-ing	-y/-ly	-er	-est
six	sixes					
tin	tins	tinned				
tip	tips	tipped	tipping		tipper	
vim						
wig	wigs					
win	wins		winning		winner	
wit	wits			witty	wittier	wittiest
yip	yips					
zip	zips	zipped	zipping		zipper	
zit	zits					

O
/ŏ/ in ox

Position: Beginning and Middle

Vocalization: Voiced

Classification: Short o

- Letter **O** can sound like **/ah/**, or it can sound like **/aw/**, or a sound that is in between the two. This can vary by dialect. Consider the two **o's** in the word **hot dog**. The **O** sound in **hot** and the **O** sound in **dog** are very different from each other.

Beginning

Base	-s/-es	-ed	-ing	-y/-ly	-er	-est
on						
ox						

Middle

Base	-s/-es	-ed	-ing	-y/-ly	-er	-est
Bob	Bob's			Bobby		
bob	bobs	bobbed	bobbing		bobber	
bog	bogs	bogged	bogging	boggy		
bop	bops	bopped	bopping			
box	boxes	boxed	boxing	boxy	boxer	
cob	cobs					
cod	cods					
cog	cogs					
con	cons	conned	conning		Conner	
cop	cops				copper	
cot	cots					
dog	dogs	dogged	dogging	doggy		
dot	dots	dotted	dotting	dotty		
fob	fobs					
fog	fogs	fogged	fogging	foggy	*foggier*	*foggiest*

O

Base	-s/-es/'s	-ed	-ing	-y/-ly	-er	-est
fox	foxes	foxed	foxing			
gob	gobs					
god	gods			godly		
God	God's			godly		
got						
hog	hogs	hogged	hogging			
hot				hotly	hotter	hottest
job	jobs					
jog	jogs	jogged	jogging		jogger	
jot	jots	jotted	jotting			
lob	lobs	lobbed	lobbing			
log	logs	logged	logging		logger	
lop	lops	lopped	lopping			
lot	lots					
lox						
mob	mobs	mobbed	mobbing			
mod	mods					
mom	moms			mommy		
Mom	Mom's			Mommy		
mop	mops	mopped	mopping			
nod	nods	nodded	nodding			
not						
pod	pods					
pop	pops	popped	popping	poppy	popper	
Pop	Pop's					
pot	pots	potted	potting		potter	
pox						
rob	robs	robbed	robbing		robber	
Rob	Rob's			Robby		
rod	rods					
rot	rots	rotted	rotting		rotter	
sob	sobs	sobbed	sobbing			
sod						
sop	sops	sopped	sopping	soppy		
tog	togs					
Tom	Tom's			Tommy		
top	tops	topped	topping		topper	
tot	tots				totter	
wok	woks					
yon						

U

/ŭ/ in up

Position: Beginning and Middle

Vocalization: Voiced

Classification: Short vowel

- **U** and **W** sometimes work as alternates. **U** will say the **/w/** sound in words with **QU** (quilt), **CU** (cuisine), **GU** (extinguish), and **SU** (suite).
- The schwa in unaccented syllables often sounds like a short **/ŭ/**, so students may frequently add **U** to multisyllable words that are spelled with other vowels.

Beginning

Base	-s/-es	-ed	-ing	-y/-ly	-er	-est
up						
us						

Middle

Base	-s/-es	-ed	-ing	-y/-ly	-er	-est
bub				Bubby		
bud	buds	budded	budding	buddy		
bug	bugs	bugged	bugging	buggy		
bun	buns					
bus	busses	bussed	bussing		busser	
but	buts	butted	butting		butter	
cub	cubs			cubby		
cud	cuds					
cup	cups	cupped	cupping			
cut	cuts		cutting		cutter	
dub	dubs	dubbed	dubbing			

22

Base	-s/-es	-ed	-ing	-y/-ly	-er	-est
dud	duds					
dug						
fun				funny	*funnier*	*funniest*
gum	gums	gummed	gumming	gummy	*gummier*	*gummiest*
gun	guns	gunned	gunning		gunner	
hub	hubs			hubby		
hug	hugs	hugged	hugging		hugger	
hum	hums	hummed	humming		hummer	
hut	huts					
jug	jugs					
lug	lugs	lugged	lugging			
mud				muddy	*muddier*	*muddiest*
mug	mugs	mugged	mugging	muggy	mugger	
nun	nuns					
nut	nuts			nutty	*nuttier*	*nuttiest*
pug	pugs					
pun	puns	punned	punning			
pup	pups			puppy		
pus						
rub	rubs	rubbed	rubbing		rubber	
rug	rugs					
run	runs		running	runny	runner	
rut	ruts	rutted				
sub	subs	subbed	subbing			
sum	sums	summed	summing		summer	
sun	suns	sunned	sunning	sunny		
tub	tubs					
tug	tugs	tugged	tugging			
tut						
tux	tuxes					
yum				yummy	*yummier*	*yummiest*

Consonants
Printable Cards

b	c
d	f

g

h

j

k

l	m
n	p

q

qu

r

s

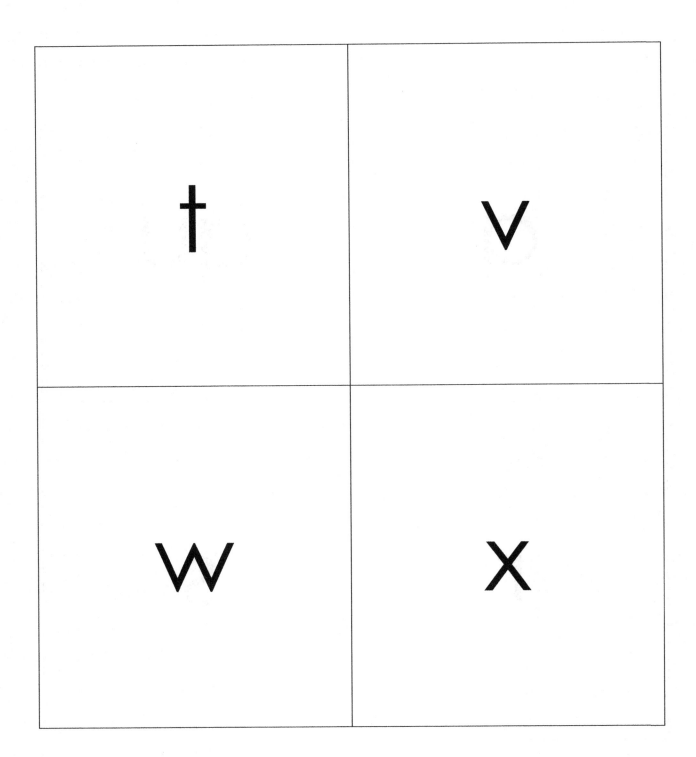

y	z

b

/b/ in bed

Position: Beginning and End

Vocalization: Voiced

Classification: Consonant

- Lowercase **b** is frequently confused with other lowercase letters **d**, **p**, and **q**, which differ only in position and not in shape.
- **B** is a part of the blends **BL** and **BR**.

Beginning

Base	-s/-es	-ed	-ing	-y/-ly	-er/-ar	-est
bad				badly		
bag	bags	bagged	bagging	baggy	bagger	
ban	bans	banned	banning		banner	
bat	bats	batted	batting	batty	batter	
bed	beds	bedded	bedding			
beg	begs	begged	begging		beggar	
bet	bets	betted	betting		better	
bib	bibs	bibbed	bibbing			
bid	bids		bidding		bidder	
big					bigger	biggest
bin	bins	binned				
bit	bits			bitty	bitter	
Bob	Bob's					
bog	bogs	bogged	bogging	boggy		
bop	bops	bopped	bopping		bopper	
bug	bugs	bugged	bugging	buggy	bugger	
bum	bums	bummed	bumming		bummer	
bun	buns			bunny		
bus	busses	bussed	bussing		busser	
but					butter	

b

Ending

Base	-s/-es/'s	-ed	-ing	-y/-ly	-er	-est
cab	cabs			cabby		
cob	cobs					
cub	cubs			cubby		
dab	dabs	dabbed	dabbing		dabber	
Deb	Deb's					
dub	dubs	dubbed	dubbing			
fob	fobs					
gab	gabs	gabbed	gabbing	gabby	gabber	
gob	gobs					
hub	hubs			hubby		
jab	jabs	jabbed	jabbing		jabber	
rub	rubs	rubbed	rubbing		rubber	
jib	jibs				jibber	
job	jobs					
lab	labs					
lob	lobs	lobbed	lobbing	lobby	lobber	
mob	mobs	mobbed	mobbing			
nab	nabs	nabbed	nabbing			
rib	ribs	ribbed	ribbing			
rob	robs	robbed	robbing		robber	
Rob				Robby		
sob	sobs	sobbed	sobbing			
sub	subs	subbed	subbing			
tab	tabs	tabbed	tabbing			
tub	tubs			tubby		
web	webs	webbed	webbing			

C

/k/ in cat

Position: Beginning

Vocalization: Unvoiced

Classification: Consonant

- **C** says its soft sound **/s/** before **E, I,** and **Y (cell, city, cyber)**. It says its hard sound **/k/** before **A, O, U (cat, cot, cut)** and all consonants **(crab, clip)**
- **C** says its hard sound when it is part of the ending syllable **-IC (terrific)**, and when it is part of the end blends **-CK (duck)** and **-CT (act)**.
- **C** is a part of the blends **CR, CL, SC,** and **SCR**.

Beginning

Base	-s/-es/'s	-ed	-ing	-y/-ly	-er	-est
cab	cabs			cabby		
Cam	Cam's					
can	cans	canned	canning		canner	
cap	caps	capped	capping			
cat	cats			catty		
cob	cobs					
cod	cods					
cog	cogs					
con	cons	conned	conning		Conner	
cop	cops				copper	
cot	cots					
cub	cubs					
cud	cuds					
cup	cups	cupped	cupping			
cut	cuts		cutting		cutter	

d

/d/ in dad

Position: Beginning, and End

Vocalization: Voiced

Classification: Consonant

- Lowercase **d** is often confused with **b, p**, and **q**, because it is different only in position, and not in shape.
- **D** is part of the suffix **-ED**. The suffix **-ED** has three sounds, including /d/ **(played)**, /ed/ **(dotted)**, and /t/ **(jumped)**.
- **D** is a part of the blends **DR** and **DW**, and end blends **ND** and **LD**.

Beginning

Base	-s/-es/'s	-ed	-ing	-y/-ly	-er	-est
dab	dabs	dabbed	dabbing		dabber	
dad	dads			daddy		
Dad	Dad's			Daddy		
dam	dams	dammed	damming			
Deb	Deb's			Debby		
den	dens					
did				diddly		
dig	digs		digging		digger	
dim	dims	dimmed	dimming	dimly	dimmer	
din					dinner	
dip	dips	dipped	dipping		dipper	
dog	dogs	dogged	dogging	doggy		
dot	dots	dotted	dotting			
Dot	Dot's			Dotty		
dub	dubs	dubbed	dubbing			
dud	duds					
dug						

Ending

Base	-s/-es/'s	-ed	-ing	-y/-ly	-er	-est
bad				badly		
bed	beds	bedded	bedding			
bid	bids		bidding		bidder	
bud	buds	budded	budding	buddy		
cod	cods					
cud	cuds					
dud	duds					
fad	fads					
fed						
god	gods			godly		
God	God's			godly		
had						
hid						
kid	kids	kidded	kidding		kidder	
lad	lads				ladder	
led						
lid	lids	lidded	lidding			
mad				madly	madder	maddest
mud				muddy	*muddier*	*muddiest*
mod	mods					
nod	nods	nodded	nodding			
pad	pads	padded	padding			
red					redder	reddest
rid						
rod	rods					
sad				sadly	sadder	saddest
sod						
Ted	Ted's			Teddy		
wad	wads	wadded	wadding			
wed	weds	wedded	wedding			

f

/f/ in fish

Position: Beginning

Vocalization: Unvoiced

Classification: Consonant

- When a word ends in the **/f/** sound, it is usually spelled **FF** (stuff). **FF** is a part of the **FLOSS** rule. See the **FF** list in the Phonogram section for **FF** words.
- **F** is a part of the blends **FR, FL**, and the end blends **LF, FT.**
- **F** and **V** sometimes work as alternates. When words ending in **F** become plural, they sometimes take on the **V** in place of the **F**. (**knife – knives, wife, wives**). This is not true for all words that end in **F** words (**roof - roofs**)
- One of the most common words is the word **of**, which pronounces the **F** as a **/v/** sound, as opposed to the word **off**, which pronounces the double **FF** as **/f/.**
- The **/f/** and **/v/** are formed in the same position of the mouth, with the only difference being that the **/f/** is unvoiced and the **/v/** is voiced.

Beginnning

Base	-s/-es	-ed	-ing	-y/-ly	-er	-est
fad	fads					
fan	fans	fanned	fanning	fanny		
fat	fats	fatted		fatty	fatter	fattest
fed						
fib	fibs	fibbed	fibbing		fibber	
fig	figs					
fin	fins	finned				
fix	fixes	fixed	fixing		fixer	
fob	fobs	fobbed	fobbing			
fog	fogs	fogged	fogging		fogger	
fox	foxes					
fun				funny	funnier	funniest

g

hard /g/ in gum

Position: Beginning and End

Vocalization: Voiced

Classification: Consonant

- **G** says its hard **/g/** sound when followed by **A, O,** and **U,** and any consonant **(gas, got, gum).** It also says its hard sound when it is located at the end of a word **(bag).**
- **G** often says its soft sound **/j/** when followed by **E, I,** or **Y,** **(gem, gist, gym)**, but it can also say its hard **/g/** sound **(get, give).**
- **G** is a part of the blends **GL** and **GR.**
- This list is for hard **/g/** only. Soft **/g/** words will be found in **Volume 2.**

Beginning

Base	-s/-es/'s	-ed	-ing	-y/-ly	-er	-est
gab	gabs	gabbed	gabbing		gabber	
gag	gags	gagged	gagging			
gal	gals					
gap	gaps					
gas	gasses			gassy	*gassier*	*gassiest*
get	gets		getting		getter	
gig	gigs					
gob	gobs					
god	gods			godly		
God	God's			godly		
got						
gum	gums	gummed	gumming			
gun	guns	gunned	gunning		gunner	

g

gum

Ending

Base	-s/-es/'s	-ed	-ing	-y/-ly	-er/-ar	-est
bag	bags	bagged	bagging	baggy	*baggier*	*baggiest*
beg	begs	begged	begging		beggar	
big					bigger	biggest
bog	bogs	bogged	bogging	boggy		
bug	bugs	bugged	bugging	buggy		
cog	cogs					
dig	digs		digging		digger	
dog	dogs	dogged	dogging	doggy		
dug						
fig	figs					
fog	fogs	fogged	fogging	foggy	fogger	
gag	gags	gagged	gagging			
gig	gigs					
hog	hogs	hogged	hogging			
hug	hugs	hugged	hugging		hugger	
jig	jigs	jigged	jigging	jiggly		
jog	jogs	jogged	jogging		jogger	
jug	jugs					
lag	lags	lagged	lagging			
leg	legs	legged	legging			
log	logs	logged	logging		logger	
lug	lugs	lugged	lugging		lugger	
mug	mugs	mugged	mugging		mugger	
nag	nags	nagged	nagging			
peg	pegs	pegged	pegging			
Peg	Peg's			Peggy		
pig	pigs			piggy		
pug	pugs					
rag	rags	ragged				
rig	rigs	rigged	rigging		rigger	
rug	rugs	rugged				
sag	sags	sagged	sagging	saggy		
tag	tags	tagged	tagging		tagger	
tog	togs					
tug	tugs	tugged	tugging			
wag	wags	wagged	wagging			
wig	wigs					

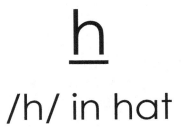

h

/h/ in hat

Position: Beginning

Vocalization: Unvoiced

Classification: Consonant

- **H** has a very consistent sound in three-letter words.
- In digraphs and other phonograms, **H** often signifies a change in sound. Some examples are **SH**, **TH**, **PH**, and **CH**.

Beginning

Base	-s/-es	-ed	-ing	-y/-ly	-er	-est
had						
ham	hams	hammed	hamming		hammer	
has						
hat	hats					
hem	hems	hemmed	hemming		hemmer	
hen	hens					
hex	hexes	hexed	hexing			
hid						
him						
hip	hips				hipper	hippest
his						
hit	hits		hitting		hitter	
hog	hogs	hogged	hogging			
hot				hotly	hotter	hottest
hub	hubs			hubby		
hug	hugs	hugged	hugging		hugger	
hum	hums	hummed	humming		Hummer	
hut	huts					

/j/ in jam

Position: Beginning

Vocalization: Voiced

Classification: Consonant

- **J** has a very consistent **/j/** sound.
- **G** can also spell the **/j/** sound when it comes before **E, I,** or **Y.**
- The letter **J** is never used at the end of a word. When there is a **/j/** sound at the end of a short vowel one-syllable word, it is spelled **DGE (fudge).** The **/j/** sound is spelled **GE** at the end of words that do not have a short vowel **(page, large, beige)**
- **J** is not usually doubled in words of English origin.
- Sometimes, the letter **D** sounds like the **/j/** sound, which may be confusing for some students. **(graduate, individual).**

Beginning

Base	-s/-es	-ed	-ing	-y/-ly	-er	-est
jab	jabs	jabbed	jabbing		jabber	
jam	jams	jammed	jamming			
jet	jets	jetted	jetting			
jib	jibs					
jig	jigs	jigged	jigging			
job	jobs					
jog	jogs	jogged	jogging		jogger	
jot	jots	jotted	jotting			
jug	jugs					

/k/ in kid

Position: Beginning

Vocalization: Unvoiced

Classification: Consonant

- **K** is used to spell the **/k/** sound before **E, I,** and **Y** (**key, kite, spunky**) That is because a **C** followed by **E, I** or **Y** will say its soft **/s/** sound **(cell, city, cyber).**
- **K** is a part of the end blend **-CK (duck).** -CK is used to spell the **/k/** sound at the end of one-syllable short vowel words. In compound words, the two words are spelled as complete words, so in compound words the **CK** may be in the middle **(duckbill).**
- Word that have vowel digraphs and r-controlled vowels spell **/k/** at the end of words with just a letter **K. (took, pork)**
- **K** is a part of the blend **SK,** which is both a beginning and end blend. It is also part of the end blends, **LK,** and **NK.** When **K** is a part of an end blend, the vowel may be either long or short.
- In long vowel words, the **K** at the end will be part of the VCE pattern (**bike, poke**), or **K** will follow a vowel team **(oak, peak).**
- **K** is not usually doubled in words of English origin. When a double might be expected, **CK** is often used.

Beginning

Base	-s/-es/'s	-ed	-ing	-y/-ly	-er	-est
Ken	Ken's					
kid	kids				kidder	
kin						
Kip	Kip's				Kipper	
Kit	Kit's					
kit	kits			kitty		

Ending

Base	-s/-es	-ed	-ing	-y/-ly	-er	-est
wok	woks					
yak	yaks	yakked	yakking			

l

/l/ in lid

Position: Beginning

Vocalization: Voiced

Classification: Consonant

- The **/l/** sound is spelled **LL** at the end of a short vowel word. This makes it part of the **FLOSS** rule.
- At the end of long vowels and multi-syllable words, only one **L** is used **(pail, beautiful)**.
- There is only one **L** in **VCE** words **(pile)**.
- **L** is a part of the blends **BL, CL, FL, GL, PL, SL, SPL,** and end blends **LD, LF, LK, LP,** and **LT,**
- The letter **L** often indicates a closed syllable exception which means that the vowel is either long or an alternative sound. **ALL, ALT, ALK, ALM, ALD, OLL, OLD, OLK,** and **OLT.**

Beginning

Base	-s/-es	-ed	-ing	-y/-ly	-er	-est
lab	labs					
lad	lads					
lag	lags	lagged	lagging			
lap	laps	lapped	lapping			
lax						
led						
leg	legs	legged				
let	lets		letting		letter	
lid	lids	lidded				
lip	lips					
lit					litter	
lob	lobs	lobbed	lobbing			

Base	-s/-es	-ed	-ing	-y/-ly	-er	-est
log	logs		logging		logger	
lop	lops	lopped	lopping			
lot	lots					
lox						
lug	lugs	lugged	lugging			

m

/m/ in mom

Position: Beginning and End

Vocalization: Voiced

Classification: Consonant

- Students sometimes confuse **M** with **W** and **N** (also **m** with **w** and **n)**.
- **M** is a part of the blend **SM** and the end blend **MP**.
- In the word family **AM**, the **M** gives a nasal quality to the letter **A**.

Beginning

Base	-s/-es/'s	-ed	-ing	-y/-ly	-er	-est
Mac	Mac's					
mad				madly	madder	maddest
man	mans	manned	manning	manly	manner	
map	maps	mapped	mapping		mapper	
Max	Max's					
men	men's					
met						
mix	mixes	mixed	mixing		mixer	
mob	mobs	mobbed	mobbing			
mod	mods					
mom	moms					
Mom	Mom's					
mop	mops	mopped	mopping			
mud				muddy	*muddier*	*muddiest*
mug	mugs	mugged	mugging		mugger	

See next page for ending M words.

Ending

Base	-s/-es/'s	-ed	-ing	-y/-ly	-er	-est
Cam	Cam's					
dam	dams	dammed	damming			
dim	dims	dimmed	dimming	dimly	dimmer	dimmest
gum	gums	gummed	gumming	gummy	*gummier*	*gummiest*
ham	hams	hammed	hamming		hammer	
hem	hems	hemmed	hemming		hemmer	
him						
jam	jams	jammed	jamming			
mom	moms			mommy		
Mom	Mom's			Mommy		
ram	rams	rammed	ramming		rammer	
sum	sums	summed	summing		summer	
vim						
yam	yams				yammer	
yum				yummy	*yummier*	*yummiest*

n
/n/ in net

Position: Beginning and End

Vocalization: Voiced

Classification: Consonant

- The letter **N** is often confused with the letter **M** (also, **n** with **m**).
- **N** is a part of the blend **SN**, and end blend **ND**.
- In the word family **AN**, the **N** gives a nasal quality to the letter **A**.

Beginning

Base	-s/-es/'s	-ed	-ing	-y/-ly	-er	-est
nab	nabs	nabbed	nabbing			
nag	nags	nagged	nagging			
Nan	Nan's					
nap	naps	napped	napping		napper	
net	nets	netted	netting			
nil						
nip	nips	nipped	nipping			
nix	nixes	nixed	nixing			
nod	nods	nodded	nodding			
not						
nun	nuns					
nut	nuts			nutty	nuttier	nuttiest

See next page for ending **N** words.

Ending

Base	-s/-es/'s	-ed	-ing	-y/-ly	-er	-est
ban	bans	banned	banning		banner	
bin	bins	binned	binning			
bun	buns			bunny		
can	cans	canned	canning	canny	canner	
con	cons	conned	conning		Conner	
den	dens					
din					dinner	
don	dons	donned	donning			
Don	Don's			Donny	Donner	
fan	fans	fanned	fanning	Fanny	fanner	
fin	fins	finned				
fun				funny	*funnier*	*funniest*
gun	guns	gunned	gunning	gunny	gunner	
hen	hens					
Ken	Ken's			Kenny		
kin						
man	man's			Manny	manner	
men	men's					
Nan	Nan's					
pan	pans	panned	panning			
pen	pens	penned	penning	penny		
pin	pins	pinned				
pun	puns	punned	punning			
ran						
run	runs		running	runny	runner	
sin	sins	sinned	sinning		sinner	
son	sons			sonny		
sun	suns	sunned	sunning	sunny	*sunnier*	*sunniest*
tan	tans	tanned	tanning		Tanner	
ten	tens					
tin	tins	tinned		tinny		
van	vans					
win	wins		winning		winner	
won						
yen						
yin						
yon						

/p/ in pig

Position: Beginning and End

Vocalization: Unvoiced

Classification: Consonant

- **P** is a part of the blends **PR, PL, SP, MP, SPL** and **SPR**.

Beginning

Base	-s/-es/'s	-ed	-ing	-y/-ly	-er	-est
pad	pads	padded	padding			
pal	pals					
pan	pans	panned	panning			
pat	pats	patted	patting		patter	
Pat	Pat's			Patty		
peg	pegs	pegged	pegging			
Peg	Peg's			Peggy		
pen	pens	penned	penning	penny		
pep				peppy	pepper	
pet	pets	petted	petting			
pic	pics					
pig	pigs	pigged	pigging	piggy		
pin	pins	pinned	pinning		pinner	
pip	pips					
pit	pits	pitted	pitting		pitter	
pod	pods					
pop	pops	popped	popping	poppy	popper	
Pop	Pop's			Poppy		
pot	pots	potted	potting	potty		

p

Base	-s/-es	-ed	-ing	-y/-ly	-er	-est
pox						
pug	pugs					
pun	puns	punned	punning			
pup	pups			puppy		
pus						

Ending

Base	-s/-es/'s	-ed	-ing	-y/-ly	-er	-est
bop	bops	bopped	bopping			
cap	caps	capped	capping			
cop	cops			copy	copper	
cup	cups	cupped	cupping			
dip	dips	dipped	dipping		dipper	
gap	gaps	gapped				
hip	hips	hipped	hipping	hippy	hipper	hippest
hop	hops	hopped	hopping		hopper	
Kip	Kip's				Kipper	
lap	laps	lapped	lapping			
lip	lips					
lop	lops	lopped	lopping		lopper	
map	maps	mapped	mapping			
mop	mops	mopped	mopping			
nap	naps	napped	napping		napper	
nip	nips	nipped	nipping			
pip	pips					
pop	pops	popped	popping		popper	
Pop	Pop's			Poppy		
pup	pups			puppy		
rap	raps	rapped	rapping		rapper	
rep	reps					
rip	rips	ripped	ripping		ripper	
sap	saps	sapped	sapping	sappy	*sappier*	*sappiest*
sip	sips	sipped	sipping	sippy	sipper	
sop	sops	sopped	sopping			
sup	sups	supped	supping		supper	
tap	taps	tapped	tapping		tapper	
top	tops	topped	topping		topper	
yap	yaps	yapped	yapping		yapper	
yip	yips	yipped	yipping	yippy		
zip	zips	zipped	zipping	zippy	zipper	

<u>qu</u>

/kw/ in quiz

Position: Beginning

Vocalization: Voiced

(**Q** as /**k**/ is not voiced, but **QU** as /**kw**/ is voiced because of the **U**)

Classification: Digraph or Blend

- **Q** is almost always paired with **U** in words of **English** origin.
- **Q** by itself makes the sound /**k**/ and is unvoiced (**Iraq**), but this only occurs in words that have been borrowed from other languages. In words of English origin, **Q** and **U** are always paired together, and say /**kw**/.
- Some educators consider **QU** to be a blend, with **Q** making the /**k**/ sound, and **U** making the /**w**/ sound. Other educators consider **QU** to be a digraph, with /**kw**/ being a unique sound.
- **U** and **W** sometimes work as alternates. **U** will say the /**w**/ sound in words with **QU** (quilt), **CU** (cuisine), **GU** (extinguish), and **SU** (suite).
- The short vowel **QU** list is very limited. You can find more **QU** words in **Volume 2** (long vowel & **CVE**).

Beginning

Base	-s/-es	-ed	-ing	-y/-ly	-er	-est
quid						
quip	quips	quipped	quipping			
quit	quits		quitting		quitter	
quiz	quizzes	quizzed	quizzing		quizzer	

See next page for **QU** words with end blends and **QU** as a part of **SQU**.

qu

QU words with end blends & SQU

Base	LT's	-s/-es	-ed	-ing	-y/-ly	-er	-est
quack	ck	quacks	quacked	quacking			
quell	ll	quells	quelled	quelling			
quick	ck				quickly	quicker	quickest
quill	ll	quills					
quilt	lt	quilts	quilted	quilting		quilter	
quint	nt						
squid	squ	squids					
squint	squ nt	squints	squinted	squinting		squinter	
squish	squ sh	squishes	squished	squishing	squishy	*squishier*	*squishiest*

r

/r/ in run

Position: Beginning

(R at the end of a word is usually a part of an **R**-controlled letter team)

Vocalization: Voiced

Classification: Consonant

- **R, S,** and **T** are the most frequent consonants in the English language.
- **R** is a part of many blends, including **BR, CR, DR, FR, GR, PR, TR, SCR, SPR,** and **STR**.
- **R** is a part of a syllable pattern called **R-controlled**, which includes **AR, ER, IR, OR,** and **UR,** and some more complex letter teams, like **EAR** in **earth**. In these syllables, **R** changes the sound of the vowel.
- This list only has beginning **R** sounds, because ending **R** sounds are usually either part of a suffix, or part of an **R-Controlled** letter team.
- Some curriculums teach that **R** is a part of end blends (such as **rl** and **rd**), but that is not correct. Most words that appear to have an **R** end blend, instead, end in an **R-Controlled** syllable, plus a consonant (c**ur**l, b**ir**d)

Beginning

rag	rags	ragged	ragging		
ram	rams	rammed	ramming		rammer
ran					
rap	raps	rapped	rapping		rapper
rat	rats	ratted	ratting	ratty	
red				redder	reddest
ref	refs				
rep	reps				
rib	ribs	ribbed	ribbing		
rid	rids		ridding		
rig	rigs			rigger	
rim	rims	rimmed			

rip	rips	ripped	ripping		ripper
rob	robs	robbed	robbing		robber
Rob	Rob's			Robby	
rod	rods				
rot	rots	rotted	rotting		
rub	rubs	rubbed	rubbing		rubber
rug	rugs				
rum					
run	runs		running	runny	runner
rut	ruts				

S̲

/s/ in sun

Position: Beginning

Vocalization: Unvoiced

Classification: Consonant

- **S** has two common sounds. The first is **/s/**, and the second is **/z/**. This list is for **/s/** words, and there is a list following this one for **/z/** words.
- **R, S,** and **T** are the most frequent consonants in the English language.
- **S** says **/s/** as a part of the **VCE** pattern **(ase)**. See **VCE** for those words.
- **S** says **/sh/** in a few words, such as **sugar** and **sure**. **S** says **/zh/** in some multi-syllable words, like **treasure** and **usual**.
- At the end of one-syllable short vowel words, **/s/** is frequently spelled **SS**. It is part of the FLOSS rule. There are a few exceptions in some common words (**his, has, is, as**). See the **FLOSS SS** list for words ending in **/s/**.
- Apostrophe **'S** is used to show possession **(Kate's).**
- **S** at the end of a word indicates a plural **(cat/cats). -ES** also indicates a plural **(peach/peaches)**
- **S** is a part of the blends **SC, SK, SL, SM, SN, SP, ST, SW, SPL, SPR, and STR** and end blends **-SK, -ST, SCR.**
- Words that end in **S** indicate a plural by doubling the last **S** and adding **-ES,** instead of **-S (bus - busses).**

Beginning

Base	-s/-es	-ed	-ing	-y/-ly	-er	-est
sag	sags	sagged	sagging	saggy		
sap	saps	sapped	sapping	sappy	*sappier*	*sappiest*
sat						
set	sets		setting		setter	
sin	sins	sinned	sinning		sinner	
sip	sips	sipped	sipping	sippy		

Base	-s/-es	-ed	-ing	-y/-ly	-er	-est
sis						
sit	sits		sitting		sitter	
six	sixes					
sob	sobs	sobbed	sobbing			
sod						
sop	sops	sopped	sopping			
sub	subs	subbed	subbing			
sum	sums	summed	summing		summer	
sun	suns	sunned	sunning	sunny	sunnier	sunniest

Ending

Base	-s/-es	-ed	-ing	-y/-ly	-er	-est
bus	busses	bussed	bussing			
gas	gasses			gassy	gassier	gassiest
pus						
sis						
us						
yes	yeses					

S says /s/ as part of suffix **-S**

The list below is only a sample. Each list in this book contains a suffix -s column.

Plural -s only says /s/ when it follows an unvoiced consonant. The rest of the time plural -S says /z/. We do this naturally when we speak, without thinking about it.

cuts	pets
gets	pops
hats	pups
hips	rats
kits	rips
laps	zips

S says **/s/** as part of apostrophe **'S**

S says **/s/** as part of apostrophe **'S** when it follows an unvoiced letter. (**S** says **/z/** when it follows a voiced letter). We do this naturally when we speak, without thinking about it.

Alf's
Art's
bat's
cap's
cat's
Dot's
Kip's
Mac's
Nat's
Pat's
pet's
pup's
Vic's

S̲

/z/ in has

Position: End

Vocalization: Voiced

Classification: Consonant

- **S** has two common sounds. The first is **/s/**, and the second is **/z/**. This is the list for **/z/** words.
- **S** does not say **/z/** at the beginning of words.
- Even though this list is short, there are many longer and multi-syllable words that have the **/z/** sound for **S**. **(cheese, music, use, present).**
- **S** makes the **/z/** sound when it is part of some plural **-S (bags)** and some plural **-ES (peaches).** See below for a sample list of **-S** and **-ES** words. Also, each list in this book has an **-S/-ES** column.
- **S** says **/z/** as a part of certain single syllable verbs (**is**) and adjectives (**his**)
- **S says /z/** as a part of some apostrophe **'S (Dave's)**.
- For **S** says **/z/** as a part of **CVE (ese, ise, ose, use),** See Volume 2.
- **S** says **/z/** as a part of words that end in **-SE (whose, please)**. See **-SE** list in Volume 3 for **-SE** words.

Beginning

as
is
has
his

See next page for more s says /z/ words.

S says **/z/** as part of suffix **-S**

S says **/z/** when it follows a voiced letter. (When it follows an unvoiced letter, it says /s/)

(There are many more words listed in the -s columns of each word list).

bags	dogs	jugs	rigs
begs	fads	kids	runs
dogs	fans	legs	tabs
bins	figs	lids	tins
bugs	fins	nods	tugs
cabs	hens	pegs	vans
cans	hogs	pigs	webs
cubs	hugs	pins	wigs
dabs	hums	rags	wins
			yams

S says **/z/** as part of the suffix **-ES.**

(There are many more words listed in the -s columns of each word list).

axes	fixes	nixes	tuxes
boxes	foxes	sixes	vexes
buses	maxes	taxes	waxes
faxes	mixes		

S says **/z/** as a part of apostrophe **'S**

S says **/z/** as a part of apostrophe **'S** when it follows a voiced letter. (**S** says **/s/** when it follows an unvoiced letter). We do this naturally when we speak, without thinking about it.

Bob's	Kim's	Cal's	Jim's
Dan's	Val's	Cam's	Sam's
Peg's	Ben's	Dan's	Tom's
dog's	Bob's	Ed's	pig's

/t/ in top

Position: Beginning and End

Vocalization: Unvoiced

Classification: Consonant

- **R, S,** and **T** are the most frequent consonants in the English language.
- **T** is a part of the blends **ST, TR, TW,** and **STR.** It is a part of the end blends **CT, FT, LT, PT, ST and TZ.**

Beginning

Base	-s/-es/'s	-ed	-ing	-y/-ly	-er	-est
tab	tabs	tabbed	tabbing			
tag	tags	tagged	tagging		tagger	
tan	tans	tanned	tanning		Tanner	
tap	taps	tapped	tapping		tapper	
tax	taxes	taxed	taxing			
Ted	Ted's			Teddy		
ten	tens					
tin	tins	tinned		tinny		
tip	tips	tipped	tipping		tipper	
tog	togs					
Tom	Tom's			Tommy		
top	tops	topped	topping		topper	
tot	tots					
tub	tubs					
tug	tugs	tugged	tugging			
tut						
tux	tuxes					

Ending

Base	-s/-es	-ed	-ing	-y/-ly	-er	-est
at						
bat	bats	batted	batting	batty	batter	
bet	bets	betted	betting		better	
bit	bits			bitty	bitter	
but	buts	butted	butting		butter	
cat	cats			catty		
cot	cots					
dot	dots	dotted	dotting			
fat	fats			fatty	fatter	fattest
fit	fits	fitted	fitting		fitter	fittest
get	gets		getting		getter	
got						
gut	guts	gutted	gutting		gutter	
hat	hats	hatted			hatter	
hit	hits		hitting		hitter	
hot				hotly	hotter	hottest
hut	huts					
it						
jet	jets	jetted	jetting			
jot	jots	jotted	jotting			
jut	juts	jutted	jutting			
kit	kits					
let	lets		letting		letter	
lit					litter	
lot	lots					
mat	mats	matted	matting		matter	
met						
net	nets	netted	netting			
not						
nut	nuts			nutty	*nuttier*	*nuttiest*
pat	pats	patted	patting		patter	
Pat				Patty		
pet	pets	petted	petting			
pit	pits	pitted	pitting		pitter	
pot	pots	potted	potting	potty	potter	
rat	rats	ratted	ratting	ratty	*rattier*	*rattiest*
rot	rots	rotted	rotting			
rut	ruts	rutted				
sat						
set	sets		setting		setter	

Base	-s/-es	-ed	-ing	-y/-ly	-er	-est
sit	sits		sitting		sitter	
tot	tots					
tut	tuts	tutted	tutting			
vat	vats					
vet	vets	vetted	vetting			
wet	wets	wetted	wetting		wetter	wettest
yet						
zit	zits					

V

/v/ in vet

Position: Beginning

Vocalization: Voiced

Classification: Consonant

- Students sometimes confuse **V** with **U** and **W** (and **v** with **u** and **w**).
- The letter **V** is not found at the end of words of English origin. For words that end in the **/v/** sound, an **E** is added (**-VE** in **give**), to prevent the **V** from being at the end of a word. This rule helps students to understand the spelling of some words, such as **have, give** and **live** that end in an **E**, but do not have a long vowel sound. See Volume 3 for **-VE** words.
- **V** is not doubled in words of English origin. This is to avoid confusion with **W**.
- **F** and **V** sometimes work as alternates. When words ending in **/f/** become plural, they sometimes take on the **V** in place of the **F**. (**knife – knives, wife, wives**).
- The **/f/** and **/v/** are formed in the same position of the mouth, with the only difference being that the **/f/** is unvoiced and the **/v/** is voiced.

Beginning

Base	-s/-es	-ed	-ing	-y/-ly	-er	-est
vac	vacs					
van	vans					
vat	vats					
vet	vets	vetted	vetting			
vex	vexes	vexed	vexing			
vim						

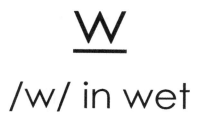

/w/ in wet

Position: Beginning

Vocalization: Voiced

Classification: Consonant

- Students sometimes confuse **W** with **M** (and **w** with **m**).
- **W** is found in less-common blends like **TW** (twist) and **DW** (dwell).
- **W** sometimes signifies a change in sound for the letters that follow **W**, such as in the phonograms **WA** (wash), **WOR** (worm) and **WAR** (warm).
- **W** is not usually doubled in words of English origin.
- **U** and **W** sometimes work as alternates. **U** will say the /**w**/ sound in words with **QU** (quilt), **CU** (cuisine), **GU** (extinguish), and **SU** (suite).

Beginning

Base	-s/-es	-ed	-ing	-y/-ly	-er	-est
wag	wags	wagged	wagging			
wax	waxes	waxed	waxing	waxy		
web	webs	webbed	webbing			
wet	wets	wetted	wetting		wetter	
wig	wigs					
win	wins		winning		winner	
wok	woks					

X

/ks/ in fox

Position: End

Vocalization: Unvoiced

Classification: Consonant

- **X** usually says **/ks/ (fox)**. However, it can also make the sound **/z/** at the beginning of words (**xylophone**), or **/gz/** (usually as part of **EX**, **exam**).
- **X** by itself is found most of the time at the end of a word. When the **/ks/** sound is found at the beginning of a word, it is usually part of **EX** (**excuse**).
- **X** is not doubled in words of English origin.
- **X** always indicates a preceding short vowel. This is because it represents two distinct sounds (Venezky, 1999)
- Words that end in **X** indicate a plural by adding **-ES**, instead of **-S (ax – axes).**

Ending

Base	-s/-es/'s	-ed	-ing	-y/-ly	-er	-est
ax	axes	axed	axing			
ox						
box	boxes	boxed	boxing	boxy	boxer	
fax	faxes	faxed	faxing			
fix	fixes	fixed	fixing		fixer	
fox	foxes	foxed	foxing			
hex	hexes	hexed	hexing			
lax					laxer	laxest
lox						
max						
Max	Max's					
mix	mixes	mixed	mixing		mixer	
nix	nixes	nixed	nixing			
pox						
sax	saxes					

Base	-s/-es	-ed	-ing	-y/-ly	-er	-est
six	sixes					
tax	taxes	taxed	taxing		taxer	
tux	tuxes					
vex	vexes	vexed	vexing			
wax	waxes	waxed	waxing	waxy		

X as part of -EX

Base	LT's	-s/-es	-ed	-ing	-y/-ly	-er	-est
duplex	pl CV	duplexes					
exact	-ct	exacts	exacted	exacting	exactly		
exam		exams					
excel	c(e)	excels	excelled	excelling			
excuse	VCE	excuses	excused	excusing		excuser	
exempt	-pt	exempts	exempted	exempting			
exert	er	exerts	exerted	exerting			
exhale	VCE	exhales	exhaled	exhaling			
exhort	or h	exhorts	exhorted	exhorting		exhorter	
exile	VCE	exiles	exiled	exiling			
exist	st	exists	existed	existing			
exit		exits	exited	exiting			
expect	-ct	expects	expected	expecting			
expel		expels	expelled	expelling		expeller	
expend	-nd	expends	expended	expending			
expert	er	experts					
expert	er	experts					
expire	ire	expires	expired	expiring			
export	or	exports	exported	exporting		exporter	
extend	-nd	extends	extended	extending		extender	
extent	-nt						
extol	*	extols	extolled	extolling			
extra	tr a	extras					
index		indexes	indexed	indexing		indexer	

Y̱

/y/ in yes

Position: Beginning

(Y at end and middle have different sounds)

Vocalization: Voiced

Classification: Consonant

(Other Y sounds may be vowels)

- Y has many sounds. See Volume 2 for the sounds of Y. The list on this page is for beginning consonant Y only. The other sounds of Y can be found in Volumes 2 and 3.
- Y works as an alternate with the letter I. Y is typically used in phonograms at the end of words, and I is typically used in the middle of words. (**boy**, **boil**), (**play**, **plait**).
- Y at the end of a word (when it is not part of a vowel team), changes to I when a vowel suffix is added (**baby, babies**).
- Y is not usually doubled in words of English origin.

Beginning

Base	-s/-es	-ed	-ing	-y/-ly	-er	-est
yak	yaks	yakked	yakking			
yam	yams				yammer	
yap	yaps	yapped	yapping		yapper	
yen	yens					
yes	yeses					
yet						
yip	yips	yipped	yipping	yippy		
yon						
yum				yummy	yummier	yummiest

Z

/z/ in zap

Position: Beginning and End

Vocalization: Voiced

Classification: Consonant

- When the **/z/** sound is found at the end of a short-vowel word, it is frequently spelled **ZZ** (**jazz**). This makes it part of the **FLOSS** rule. See the **ZZ** phonogram list for **ZZ** words. There are several exceptions to this rule (**quiz**)
- **/z/** is also found at the end of words in the **VCE** pattern (**haze**), and in root words as a part of a consonant blend (**waltz, pretzel**)

One-syllable

Base	-s/-es	-ed	-ing	-y/-ly	-er	-est
fez						
quiz	quizzes	quizzed	quizzing		quizzer	
zap	zaps	zapped	zapping		zapper	
zip	zips	zipped	zipping	zippy	zipper	
zit	zits					

Z (with advanced sounds)

Base		-s/-es	-ed	-ing	-y/-ly	-er	-est
blitz	tz	blitzes	blitzed	blitzing		blitzer	
glitz	tz				glitzy	glitzier	glitziest
hertz	tz						
quiz	qu	quizzes	quizzed	quizzing		quizzer	
whiz	wh	whizzes	whizzed	whizzing			
zest	st				zesty	zestier	zestiest
zing	ng	zings				zinger	
zoo	oo	zoos					

67

FLOSS (End doubles)
– Printable Cards

ff	ll
ss	zz

ff

/f/ in off

Position: End

Vocalization: Unvoiced

Classification: End Blend

Group: FLOSS

- **FF** follows the **FLOSS** rule. **F, L, S**, and **Z** are usually doubled at the end of a one-syllable short-vowel word.
- The words **OFF** and **OF** are often confusing to students. The word **OFF** follows the **FLOSS** rules, but the word **OF** does not. **F** and **V** are sometimes used as alternates, and the **F** in **OF** says the /**v**/ sound.

Base	LT's	-s/-es	-ed	-ing	-y/-ly	-er	-est
bluff	bl	bluffs	bluffed	bluffing			
chaff	ch						
fluff	fl	fluffs	fluffed	fluffing	fluffy	fluffier	fluffiest
gruff	gr				gruffly	gruffer	gruffest
huff		huffs	huffed	huffing	huffy	huffier	huffiest
jiff					jiffy		
off						offer	
puff		puffs	puffed	puffing	puffy	puffier	puffiest
scoff	sc	scoffs	scoffed	scoffing		scoffer	
scuff	sc	scuffs	scuffed	scuffing			
sniff	sn	sniffs	sniffed	sniffing	sniffy	sniffer	
staff	st	staffs	staffed	staffing		staffer	
stuff	st	stuffs	stuffed	stuffing	stuffy	stuffer	
tiff							

Compound

Base	LT's	-s/-es	-ed	-ing	-y/-ly	-er	-est
castoff	st						
clifftop	cl	clifftops					
cufflink	ink	cufflinks					
cutoff		cutoffs					
Flagstaff	fl st						
foodstuff	st oo	foodstuffs					
handcuff	nd	handcuffs					
kickoff	ck	kickoffs					
knockoff	kn ck	knockoffs					
layoff	ay	layoffs					
offbeat	ea						
offhand	nd		offhanded				
offline	i-e						
offload	oa	offloads	offloaded	offloading			
offset		offsets		offsetting			
offshoot	sh oo	offshoots					
offshore	sh o-e						
offstage	st age						
payoff	ay	payoffs					
puffball	all	puffballs					
showoff	sh ow	showoffs					
standoff	st nd	standoffs					
takeoff	a-e	takeoffs					

/l/ in hill

Position: End

Vocalization: Voiced

Classification: End Blend

Group: FLOSS

- **LL** follows the **FLOSS** rule. **F, L, S**, and **Z** are usually doubled at the end of a one-syllable short-vowel word. There are some exceptions to this rule.
- Words with the phonogram **ALL** are not considered part of the FLOSS rule. **ALL** is a separate phonogram.
- When words that end in **LL** are joined to be a part of a multisyllable word, the second **L** is frequently dropped. **(beauty+full = beautiful, well + fare = welfare).** However, many compound words retain the **LL** **(base+ball=baseball).**
- **OLL** and **ALL** words are listed in the Closed Syllable Exceptions section.

Base		-s/-es/'s	-ed	-ing	-y/-ly	-er/-ar	-est
bell		bells	belled	belling			
bill		bills	billed	billing		biller	
Bill		Bill's			Billy		
cell	c(e)	cells				cellar	
chill	ch	chills	chilled	chilling	chilly	chillier	chilliest
cull		culls	culled	culling			
dell		dells					
Dell		Dell's					
dill					dilly		
doll		dolls			dolly	dollar	
drill	dr	drills	drilled	drilling		driller	
dull						duller	dullest
dwell	dw	dwells	dwelled	dwelling		dweller	
fell		fells	felled	felling			

Base	-s/-es	-ed	-ing	-y/-ly	-er	-est
fill		fills	filled	filling		filler	
frill	fr	frills	frilled	frilling	frilly	frillier	frilliest
gill		gills					
gull		gulls					
hell							
hill		hills			hilly	hillier	hilliest
hull		hulls	hulled	hulling			
ill		ills					
Jill		Jill's					
lull		lulls	lulled	lulling			
mill		mills	milled	milling		Miller	
mull		mulls	mulled	mulling			
Nell		Nell's			Nelly		
pill		pills	pilled	pilling			
pull	u	pulls	pulled	pulling	pully	puller	
quell	qu	quells	quelled	quelling			
quill	qu	quills	quilled	quilling			
shell	sh	shells	shelled	shelling	Shelly		
sill		sills			silly	sillier	silliest
skill	sk	skills	skilled				
skull	sk	skulls					
smell	sm	smells	smelled	smelling	smelly	smellier	smelliest
spell	sp	spells	spelled	spelling		speller	
spill	sp	spills	spilled	spilling		spiller	
still	st	stills	stilled	stilling		stiller	stillest
swell	sw	swells	swelled	swelling			
swill	sw	swills	swilled	swilling			
tell		tells		telling		teller	
till		tills				tiller	
twill	tw	twills					
well		wells	welled	welling			
will		wills	willed	willing			
Will		Will's			Willy		
yell		yells	yelled	yelling		yeller	

See next page for LL compound words.

Compound

Base	-s/-es	-ed	-ing	-y/-ly	-er	-est
barbell	ar	barbells				
bedroll	oll	bedrolls				
bellboy	oy	bellboys				
bellhop		bellhops				
billfold	old	billfolds				
bulldog	u	bulldogs				
bullfrog	u fr	bullfrogs				
bullhorn	u or	bullhorns				
bullwhip	u wh	bullwhips				
cellmate	a-e c(e)	cellmates				
cowbell	ow	cowbells				
doorbell	oor	doorbells				
downhill	ow					
dumbbell	mb	dumbbells				
eggshell	gg* sh	eggshells				
farewell	a-e	farewells				
foothill	oo	foothills				
goodwill	oo					
handbill	nd	handbills				
hillside	i-e	hillsides				
hilltop		hilltops				
inkwell	ink	inkwells				
killjoy	oy					
landfill	nd	landfills				
molehill	o-e					
outsell	ou	outsells	outselling			
overall	er					
overkill	er	overkills				
pillbox		pillboxes				
playbill	pl ay	playbills				
sawmill	aw	sawmills				
seagull	ea	seagulls				

SS

/s/ in cross

Position: End

Vocalization: Unvoiced

Classification: End Blend

Group: FLOSS

- SS follows the **FLOSS** rule. **F, L, S**, and **Z** are usually doubled at the end of a one-syllable short-vowel word. There are some exceptions to this rule.
- The double **SS** indicates that the word ending in **S** is not plural.
- Words that end in **SS** indicate a plural by adding -**ES**, instead of -**S** (**bless** - **blesses**).

Base	-s/-es/'s	-ed	-ing	-y/-ly	-er	-est
bass						
Bess		Bess's			Bessy	
bless	bl	blesses	blessed	blessing		
bliss	bl					
boss		bosses	bossed	bossing	bossy	bossier	bossiest
chess	ch					
class	cl	classes	classed	classing	classy	classier	classiest
cross	cr	crosses	crossed	crossing	crossly		
dress	dr	dresses	dressed	dressing	dressy	dresser	
fess		fesses	fessed	fessing			
floss	fl	flosses	flossed	flossing	Flossy	flosser	
fuss		fusses	fussed	fussing	fussy	fussier	fussiest
glass	gl	glasses	glassed	glassing	glassy	glassier	glassiest
gloss	gl	glosses	glossed	glossing	glossy	glossier	glossiest
grass	gr	grasses			grassy	grassier	grassiest
gross	gr ō*				grossly	grosser	grossest
hiss		hisses	hissed	hissing	hissy		
kiss		kisses	kissed	kissing	kissy	kisser	

74

Base	-s/-es/'s	-ed	-ing	-y/-ly	-er	-est
lass	lasses					
less					lesser	
loss	losses					
mass	masses	massed	massing			
mess	messes	messed	messing	messy	*messier*	*messiest*
miss	misses	missed	missing			
moss	mosses			mossy	*mossier*	*mossiest*
muss	musses	mussed	mussing	mussy	*mussier*	*mussiest*
pass	passes	passed	passing		passer	
press	pr	presses	pressed	pressing	presser	
Ross	Ross's					
sass	sasses	sassed	sassing	sassy	*sassier*	*sassiest*
toss	tosses	tossed	tossing			

Compound

Base	LT's	-s/-es	-ed	-ing	-y/-ly	-er	-est
ageless	a-e ge						
backless	ck						
badness							
baseless	a-e				baselessly		
blameless	bl a-e				blamelessly		
bloodless	bl oo						
boundless	ou -nd				boundlessly		
brainless	br ai				brainlessly		
cesspool	oo c(e)	cesspools					
cheerless	ch ee				cheerlessly		
chessmen	ch						
childless	ch ild						
classmate	cl a-e	classmates					
classroom	cl oo	classrooms					
cloudless	cl ou						
clueless	cl ue				cluelessly		
colorless	or				colorlessly		
crabgrass	cr gr						
crossbar	cr ar	crossbars					
crossbow	cr ow	crossbows					
crossfire	cr i-e						
crossover	cr er ō						
crosstown	cr ow						
crosswalk	cr alk	crosswalks					

Base	LT's	-s/-es/'s	-ed	-ing	-y/-ly	-er	-est
crossword	cr wor	crosswords					
doubtless	ou bt				doubtlessly		
dreamless	dr ea				dreamlessly		
endless	nd				endlessly		
eyeglass	eye* gl	eyeglasses					
faceless	a-e ce						
faithless	ai th				faithlessly		
flawless	fl aw				flawlessly		
formless	or				formlessly		
fruitless	fr ui				fruitlessly		
fusspot		fusspots					
glassware	gl a-e						
godless					godlessly		
grandness	gr nd						
grassland	gr nd	grasslands					
grossness	gr ō						
guesswork	wor gue						
hairless	ai						
harmless	ar				harmlessly		
heartless	ear*				heartlessly		
homeless	o-e						
hopeless	o-e				hopelessly		
humorless	or				humorlessly		
landless	nd						
landmass	nd	landmasses					
lawless	aw				lawlessly		
lifeless	i-e						
mindless	ind				mindlessly		
needless	ee				needlessly		
noiseless	oi se				noiselessly		
outclass	ou cl	outclasses	outclassed	outclassing			
outguess	ou gue	outguesses	outguessed	outguessing			
overpass	er	overpasses					
painless	ai				painlessly		
passbook	oo	passbooks					
passkey	ey	passkeys					
passport	or	passports					
password	or	passwords					

Base	LT's	-s/-es/'s	-ed	-ing	-y/-ly	-er	-est
peerless	ee						
seamless	ea				seamlessly		
seedless	ee						
selfless	lf				selflessly		
skinless	sk						
spotless	sp				spotlessly		
starless	st ar						
sundress	dr	sundresses					
sunless							
tactless	ct				tactlessly		
timeless	i-e				timelessly		
toneless	o-e				tonelessly		
useless	u-e				uselessly		
windless	nd						
wireless	i-e				wirelessly		
wordless	or				wordlessly		

ZZ

/z/ in buzz

Position: End

Vocalization: Voiced

Classification: End Blend

Group: FLOSS

- **ZZ** follows the **FLOSS** rule. **F, L, S,** and **Z** are usually doubled at the end of a one-syllable short-vowel word. There are some exceptions to this rule, especially for the letter **Z**.

Base		-s/-es	-ed	-ing	-y/-ly	-er	-est
buzz		buzzes	buzzed	buzzing	buzzy	buzzier	buzziest
fizz		fizzes	fizzed	fizzing	fizzy	fizzier	fizziest
frizz	fr	frizzes	frizzed	frizzing	frizzy	frizzier	frizziest
fuzz		fuzzes	fuzzed	fuzzing	fuzzy	fuzzier	fuzziest
jazz		jazzes	jazzed	jazzing	jazzy	jazzier	jazziest
razz		razzes	razzed	razzing			
whizz	wh	whizzes	whizzed	whizzing	whizzy	whizzier	whizziest

Compound

Base	LT's	-s/-es	-ed	-ing	-y/-ly	-er	-est
buzzword	wor	buzzwords					

See next page for ZZ Multisyllable Words.

Multi-syllable

Base		-s/-es	-ed	-ing	-y/-ly	-er	-est
buzzard	ar	buzzards					
drizzly	dr -ly						
gizzard	ar	gizzards					
grizzly	gr -ly	grizzlies					
scuzzy	sc -y					scuzzier	scuzziest
snazzy	sn -y					snazzier	snazziest

L-Blends

Printable Cards

bl	cl
fl	gl

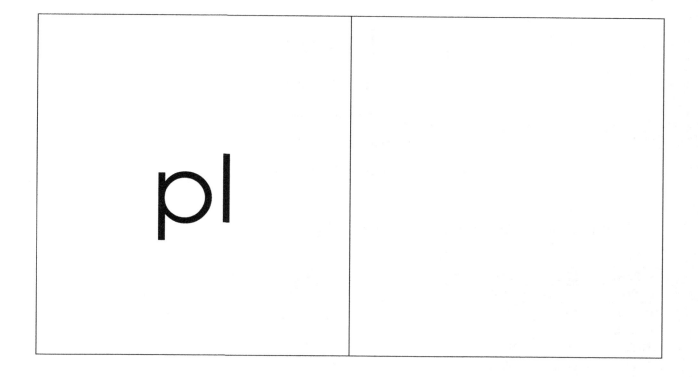

bl

/bl/ in bless

Position: Beginning

Vocalization: Voiced

Classification: Blend

Group: L-Blends

- **BL** is a blend. The **B** and **L** retain their original sounds.

Base	LT's	-s/-es/'s	-ed	-ing	-y/-ly	-er	-est
blab		blabs	blabbed	blabbing	blabby	blabber	
black	ck					blacker	blackest
blade	a-e	blades					
Blair	air	Blair's					
Blake	a-e	Blake's					
blame	a-e	blames	blamed	blaming		blamer	
blanch	nch	blanches	blanched	blanching			
bland	nd				blandly	blander	
blank	ank	blanks	blanked	blanking	blankly	blanker	blankest
blare	a-e	blares	blared	blaring			
blast	st	blasts	blasted	blasting		blaster	
blaze	a-e	blazes	blazed	blazing			
bleak	ea				bleakly	bleaker	bleakest
bleat	ea	bleats	bleated	bleating			
bled							
bleed	ee	bleeds		bleeding		bleeder	
blend	nd	blends	blended	blending		blender	
bless	ss	blesses	blessed	blessing			
blew	ew						
blight	ight	blights	blighted				
blimp	mp	blimps					
blind	ind	blinds	blinded	blinding	blindly	blinder	blindest
blink	ink	blinks	blinked	blinking		blinker	

Base	LT's	-s/-es/'s	-ed	-ing	-y/-ly	-er	-est
blip		blips	blipped	blipping			
bliss	ss						
blitz	tz	blitzes	blitzed	blitzing		blitzer	
blob		blobs					
bloke	o-e	blokes					
blood	oo				bloody	*bloodier*	*bloodiest*
bloom	oo	blooms	bloomed	blooming		bloomer	
blot		blots	blotted	blotted		blotter	
blow	ow	blows		blowing	blowy	blower	
blown	ow						
blue	ue					bluer	bluest
bluff	ff	bluffs	bluffed	bluffing		bluffer	
blunt	nt	blunts	blunted	blunting	bluntly	blunter	bluntest
blur	ur	blurs	blurred	blurring	blurry		
blurt	ur	blurts	blurted	blurting			
blush	sh	blushes	blushed	blushing			

See next page for **BL** compound words.

Compound

Base	LT's	-s/-es	-ed	-ing	-y/-ly
Compound					
blackbird	ck ir	blackbirds			
blackboard	ck oar	blackboards			
blackjack	ck				
blacklist	st	blacklists	blacklisted	blacklisting	
blackmail	ck ai	blackmails	blackmailed	blackmailing	
blackout	ck ou	blackouts			
blacksmith	ck sm th	blacksmiths			
blacktop	ck	blacktops			
blameless	a-e ss				blamelessly
blowhard	ow ar	blowhards			
blowtorch	ow or ch	blowtorches			
blowup	ow	blowups			
bluebell	ue ll	bluebells			
bluebird	ue ir	bluebirds			
bluegrass	ue gr ss				
blue jay	ue ay	blue jays			
blueprint	ue pr nt	blueprints			
lifeblood	i-e oo				
nosebleed	o-e ee	nosebleeds			
roadblock	oa ck	roadblocks			
sandblast	nd st	sandblasts	sandblasted	sandblasting	
sunblock	ck				
windblown	nd ow				
woodblock	oo ck	woodblocks			

cl

/kl/ in class

Position: Beginning

Vocalization: Voiced

Classification: Blend

Group: L-Blends

- **CL** is a blend. The **C** and **L** retain their original sounds.

Base	LT's	-s/-es/'s	-ed	-ing	-y/-ly	-er	-est
clack	ck	clacks	clacked	clacking		clacker	
clad							
claim	ai	claims	claimed	claiming			
Claire	e* air	Claire's					
clam		clams	clammed	clamming	clammy		
clamp	mp	clamps	clamped	clamping			
clang	ang	clangs	clanged	clanging			
clank	ank	clanks	clanked	clanking			
clap		claps	clapped	clapping		clapper	
Clark	ar	Clark's					
clash	sh	clashes	clashed	clashing		clasher	
clasp	sp	clasps	clasped	clasping			
class	ss	classes	classed	classing	classy	*classier*	*classiest*
Claude	e* au	Claude's					
Claus	au						
clause	au se	clauses					
claw	aw	claws	clawed	clawing			
clay	ay	clays					
Clay	ay	Clay's					
clean	ea	cleans	cleaned	cleaning	cleanly	cleaner	cleanest
clear	ear	clears	cleared	clearing	clearly	clearer	clearest
cleat	ea	cleats					
clef							

cl

Base	LT's	-s/-es/'s	-ed	-ing	-y/-ly	-er	-est
cleft	ft						
clench	nch	clenches	clenched	clenching		clencher	
clerk	er	clerks	clerked	clerking			
click	ck	clicks	clicked	clicking		clicker	
cliff	ff	cliffs					
Cliff	ff	Cliff's					
climb	mb	climbs	climbed	climbing		climber	
clinch	nch	clinches	clinched	clinching		clincher	
cling	ing	clings		clinging	clingy	*clingier*	*clingiest*
clink	ink	clinks	clinked	clinking		clinker	
Clint	nt	Clint's					
clip		clips	clipped	clipping		clipper	
Clive	i-e	Clive's					
cloak	oa	cloaks	cloaked	cloaking			
clock	ck	clocks	clocked	clocking		clocker	
clod							
clog		clogs	clogged	clogging			
close	o-e	closes	closed	closing		closer	
clot		clots	clotted	clotting		clotter	
cloth	th	clothes	clothed	clothing			
cloud	ou	clouds	clouded	clouding	cloudy		
clove	o-e	cloves				clover	
Clove	o-e	Clove's					
clown	ow	clowns	clowned	clowning			
club		clubs	clubbed	clubbing			
cluck	ck	clucks	clucked	clucking			
clue	ue	clues	clued	cluing			
clump	mp	clumps	clumped	clumping	clumpy	*clumpier*	*clumpiest*
clung	ung						
clunk	unk	clunks	clunked	clunking	clunky	clunker	
clutch	tch	clutches	clutched	clutching			
Clyde	y-e	Clyde's					

See next page for **CL** compound words.

Compound

Base	LT's	-s/-es	-ed	-ing	-y/-ly	-er	-est
clapboard	oar						
claptrap	tr						
classmate	ss a-e	classmates					
classroom	ss oo	classrooms					
cleanup	ea						
clifftop	ff	clifftops					
clipboard	oar	clipboards					
clockwise	ck i-e						
clockwork	ck wor						
closeout	o-e ou	closeouts					
clothespin	th -s o-e	clothespins					
clubhouse	ou se	clubhouses					
clueless	ue ss				cluelessly		
dishcloth	sh th						
nightclub	ight	nightclubs					
oilcloth	th oi						
outclass	ou cl ss	outclasses	outclassed	outclassing			
salesclerk	a-e er	salesclerks					

f̲l̲

/fl/ in flag

Position: Beginning

Vocalization: Voiced

Classification: Blend

Group: L-Blends

- **FL** is a blend.. The **F** and **L** retain their original sounds.

Base	LT's	-s/-es/'s	-ed	-ing	-y/-ly	-er	-est
flab					flabby	*flabbier*	*flabbiest*
flack	ck						
flag		flags	flagged	flagging		flagger	
flail	ai	flails	flailed	flailing			
flair	air	flairs					
flake	a-e	flakes	flaked	flaking	flaky	flaker	
flame	a-e	flames	flamed	flaming			
flank	ank	flanks	flanked	flanking		flanker	
flap		flaps	flapped	flapping	flappy	flapper	
flare	are	flares	flared	flaring			
flash	sh	flashed	flashed	flashing	flashy	flasher	
flask	sk	flasks					
flat		flats			flatly	flatter	flattest
flaunt	au nt	flaunts	flaunted	flaunting		flaunter	
flaw	aw	flaws	flawed				
flax							
flay	ay	flays	flayed	flaying			
flea	ea	fleas					
fleck	ck	flecks	flecked	flecking			
fled							
flee	ee	flees		fleeing			
fleet	ee	fleets	fleeted	fleeting	fleetly	fleeter	fleetest

flew	ew					
flex		flexes	flexed	flexing		
flick	ck	flicks	flicked	flicking		flicker
flight	ight	flights	flighted	flighting	flighty	fighter
fling	ing	flings		flinging		flinger
flint	nt	flints				
flip		flips	flipped	flipping	flippy	flipper
flirt	ir	flirts	flirted	flirting	flirty	flirter
flit		flits	flitted	flitting		flitter
float	oa	floats	floated	floating	floaty	floater
flock	ck	flocks	flocked	flocking		
flog		flogs	flogged	flogging		flogger
flood	oo	floods	flooded	flooding		
floor	oor	floors	floored	flooring		
flop		flops	flopped	flopping	floppy	flopper
floss	ss	flosses	flossed	flossing		flosser
flour	ou	flours	floured	flouring	floury	
flout	ou	flouts	flouted	flouting		flouter
flow	ow	flows	flowed	flowing	flowy	flower
Floyd	oy	Floyd's				
flub		flubs	flubbed	flubbing		
flue	ue	flues				
fluke	u-e	flukes				
flung	ung					
flunk	unk	flunks	flunked	flunking		
flush	sh	flushes	flushed	flushing		flusher
flute	u-e	flutes	fluted	fluting		
flux						
fly	y	flies		flying		flier
Flynn	y	Flynn's				

Compound

Base	LT's	-s/-es	-ed	-ing	-y/-ly	-er	-est
firefly	ire y	fireflies					
flagpole	o-e	flagpoles					
Flagstaff	st ff						
flapjack	ck	flapjacks					
flashback	sh ck	flashbacks					
flashbulb	sh	flashbulbs					
flashlight	sh ight	flashlights					
flashpoint	sh oi nt	flashpoints					
flatbed		flatbeds					
flatcar	ar	flatcars					
fleabite	ea i-e	fleabites					
flintlock	nt ck	flintlocks					
floodgate	oo a-e	floodgates					
flophouse	ou se	flophouses					
flywheel	y wh ee	flywheels					
horsefly	or se y	horseflies					
mudflap		mudflaps					
newsflash	ew sh	newsflashes					
outflank	ou ank	outflanks	outflanked	outflanking			
overflow	er ow	overflows	overflowed	overflowing			
skinflint	sk nt	skinflints					
snowflake	sn ow a-e	snowflakes					

gl

/gl/ in glass

Position: Beginning

Vocalization: Voiced

Classification: Blend

Group: L-Blends

- **GL** is a blend. The **G** and **L** retain their original sounds.

Base	LT's	-s/-es	-ed	-ing	-y/-ly	-er	-est
glad					gladly	gladder	gladdest
glade	a-e	glades					
glance	c(e)	glances	glanced	glancing			
gland	nd	glands					
glare	a-e	glares	glared	glaring		glarer	
glass	ss	glasses	glassed	glassing	glassy		
gleam	ea	gleams	gleamed	gleaming			
glean	ea	gleans	gleaned	gleaning		gleaner	
glee	ee						
glen		glens					
Glen		Glen's					
glib					glibly		
glide	i-e	glides	glided	gliding		glider	
glint	nt	glints	glinted	glinting			
gloat	oa	gloats	gloated	gloating		gloater	
glob		globs					
globe	o-e	globes					
gloom	oo				gloomy	gloomier	gloomiest
glop		glops	glopped	glopping	gloppy		
gloss	ss	glosses	glossed	glossing	glossy	glossier	glossiest
glove	ove*	globes	gloved	gloving			
glow	ow	glows	glowed	glowing			

glue	ue	glues	glued	gluing		gluer	
glum					glumly	glummer	glummest
glut		gluts	glutted	glutting			

Compound

Base	LT's	-s/-es	-ed	-ing	-y/-ly	-er	-est
eyeglass	eye* gl	eyeglasses					
hourglass	our gl ss	hourglasses					

pl

/pl/ in play

Position: Beginning

Vocalization: Voiced

Classification: Blend

Group: L-Blends

- **PL** is a blend. The **P** and **L** retain their original sounds.

Base	LT's	-s/-es	-ed	-ing	-y/-ly	-er	-est
plan		plans	planned	planning		planner	
plane	a-e	planes	planed				
plank	ank	planks	planked	planking			
plant	nt	plants	planted	planting		planter	
play	ay	plays	played	playing		player	
plea	ea	pleas					
plead	ea	pleads	pleaded	pleading		pleader	
pleat	ea	pleats	pleated	pleating			
pled							
pledge	dge	pledges	pledged	pledging			
plod		plods	plodded	plodding			
plop		plops	plopped	plopping			
plot		plots	plotted	plotting		plotter	
ploy	oy	ploys					
pluck	ck	plucks	plucked	plucking	plucky	pluckier	pluckiest
plug		plugs	plugged	plugging			
plum		plums					
plump	mp	plumps	plumped	plumping		plumper	plumpest
plunk	unk	plunks	plunked	plunking			
plus		plusses	plussed				
plush	sh					plusher	plushest

Compound

Base	LT's	-s/-es/'s	-ed	-ing	-y/-ly
airplane	air a-e	airplanes			
downplay	ow ay	downplays	downplayed	downplaying	
earplug	ear	earplugs			
eggplant	nt	eggplants			
fireplace	ire a-e c(e)	fireplaces			
helpless	lp ss				helplessly
hotplate	a-e	hotplates			
outplay	ou ay	outplays	outplayed	outplaying	
platform	or	platforms			
playback	ay ck	playbacks			
playbill	ay ll	playbills			
playgroup	ay gr ou	playgroups			
playhouse	ay ou se	playhouses			
playpen	ay	playpens			
playroom	ay oo	playrooms			
plaything	ay th ing	playthings			
playtime	ay i-e	playtimes			
plywood	y (my) oo				
snowplow	sn ow	snowplows			
warplane	war a-e	warplanes			
wordplay	wor ay	wordplays			

S Blends– Printable Cards

sc	sk
sl	sm

sn

sp

st

sw

SC

/sk/ in scale

Position: Beginning

Vocalization: Unvoiced

Classification: Blend

Group: S-Blends

- **SC** is a blend. The **S** and **C** retain their original sounds.
- **SC** has two sounds. It says **/sk/** when it precedes most letters. **SC** says **/s/** before the letters **E**, **I**, and **Y**, following the rules for letter **C**.
- Sc says **/s/** in words that come from Greek. See the **SC** in scent list in Volume 2 (short **C** section) for those words.

Base	LT's	-s/-es	-ed	-ing	-y/-ly	-er	-est
scab		scabs	scabbed	scabbing	scabby		
scale	a-e	scales	scaled	scaling	scaly	scalier	scaliest
scalp	lp	scalps	scalped	scalping		scalper	
scam		scams	scammed	scamming		scammer	
scamp	mp	scamps				scamper	
scan		scans	scanned	scanning		scanner	
scant	nt				scanty		
scar	ar	scars	scarred	scarring			
scare	a-e	scares	scared	scaring	scary	scarier	scariest
scarf	ar	scarves	scarfed	scarfing			
scat						scatter	
scoff	ff	scoffs	scoffed	scoffing		scoffer	
scold	old	scolds	scolded	scolding		scolder	
scone	o-e	scones					
scoop	oo	scoops	scooped	scooping		scooper	
scoot	oo	scoots	scooted	scooting		scooter	

Base	LT's	-s/-es/'s	-ed	-ing	-y/-ly	-er	-est
scope	o-e	scopes	scoped	scoping			
scorch	or ch	scorches	scorched	scorching		scorcher	
score	o-e	scores	scored	scoring		scorer	
scorn	or	scorns	scorned	scorning			
Scott	tt*	Scott's					
scour	ou	scours	scoured	scouring			
scout	ou	scouts	scouted	scouting		scouter	
scowl	ow	scowls	scowled	scowling			
scuff	ff	scuffs	scuffed	scuffing			
sculpt	lp/pt	sculpts	sculpted	sculpting			
scum					*scummy*	*scummier*	*scummiest*

Compound

Base	LT's	-s/-es	-ed	-ing	-y/-ly
downsize	ow i-e	downsizes	downsized	downsizing	
landscape	nd a-e	landscapes			
limescale	i-e a-e				
moonscape	oo a-e	moonscapes			
scapegoat	a-e oa	scapegoats			
scarecrow	a-e cr ow	scarecrows			
scorecard	ore ar	scorecards			
scoreless	ore ss				
seascape	ea a-e	seascapes			

sk
/sk/ in skate

Position: Beginning and End

(See -SK for /sk/ at the end of words)

Vocalization: Unvoiced

Classification: Blend

Group: S-Blends

- **SK** is a blend. The **S** and **K** retain their original sounds.
- This list is for **SK** as a beginning sound. See **SK** in the End Blends section for more **SK** words.

Base	LT's	-s/-es	-ed	-ing	-y/-ly	-er	-est
skate	a-e	skates	skated	skating		skater	
sketch	tch	sketches	sketched	sketching		sketcher	
skew	ew	skews	skewed	skewing		skewer	
ski	i*	skis	skied	skiing		skier	
skid		skids	skidded	skidding		skidder	
skill	ll	skills	skilled				
skim		skims	skimmed	skimming		skimmer	
skin		skins	skinned	skinning	skinny	*skinnier*	*skinniest*
skip		skips	skipped	skipping		skipper	
skirt	ir	skirts	skirted	skirting			
skit		skits				skitter	
skull	ll	skulls					
skunk	unk	skunks					
sky	y	skies					

See the next page for **SK** compound words.

Compound Words

Base	LT's	-s/-es/'s	-ed	-ing	-y/-ly	-er	-est
skateboard	a-e oar	skateboards					
sketchbook	tch oo	sketchbooks					
sketchpad	tch	sketchpads					
skincare	are						
skinless	ss						
skycap	y	skycaps					
skyjack	y ck	skyjacks					
skylark	y ar	skylarks					
skyline	y i-e	skylines					

sl

/sl/ in sled

Position: Beginning

Vocalization: Voiced

Classification: Blend

Group: L-Blends

- **SL** is a blend. **S** and **L** retain their original sounds.

Base	LT's	-s/-es/'s	-ed	-ing	-y/-ly	-er	-est
slab		slabs	slabbed	slabbing			
slack	ck	slacks	slacked	slacking		slacker	
Slade	a-e	Slade's					
slain	ai						
slam		slams	slammed	slamming		slammer	
slang	ang						
slant	nt	slants	slanted	slanting			
slap		slaps	slapped	slapping		slapper	
slash	sh	slashes	slashed	slashing		slasher	
slat		slats	slatted				
slate	a-e	slates	slated				
slave	a-e	slaves	slaved	slaving			
slaw	aw						
slay	ay	slays	slayed	slaying		slayer	
sled		sleds	sledded	sledding		sledder	
sleek	ee				sleekly	sleeker	sleekest
sleep	ee	sleeps		sleeping	sleepy	sleeper	
sleet	ee	sleets	sleeted	sleeting			
sleeve	ee ve	sleeves					
sleigh	eigh	sleighs					
slept	pt						
slew	ew						

Base	LT's	-s/-es/'s	-ed	-ing	-y/-ly	-er	-est
slice	i-e	slices	sliced	slicing		slicer	
slick	ck				slickly	slicker	slickest
slide	i-e	slides		sliding		slider	
slight	ight	slights	slighted	slighting	slightly		
slim						slimmer	slimmest
slime	i-e	slimes	slimed	sliming	slimy	*slimier*	*slimiest*
sling	ing	slings		slinging			
slip		slips	slipped	slipping		slipper	
slit		slits	slitted	slitting			
Sloan	oa	Sloan's					
slob		slobs				slobber	
slog		slogs	slogged	slogging			
sloop	oo	sloops					
slop		slops	slopped	slopping	sloppy	*sloppier*	*sloppiest*
slope	o-e	slopes	sloped	sloping			
slosh	sh	sloshes	sloshed	sloshing			
slot		slots	slotted	slotting			
sloth	th	sloths					
slouch	ou ch	slouches	slouched	slouching			
slows	ow	slows	slowed	slowing	slowly	slower	slowest
slum		slums	slummed	slumming			
slump	mp	slumps	slumped	slumping			
slung	ung						
slunk	unk						
slur	ur	slurs	slurred	slurring			
slurp	ur	slurps	slurped	slurping	slurpy	*slurpier*	*slurpiest*
sly	y				slyly	slyer	slyest

Compound

backslide	ck i-e	backslides		backsliding
bobsled		bobsleds		
bobsleigh	eigh	bobsleighs		
coleslaw	o-e sl aw			
dogsled		dogsleds		
mudslide	i-e	mudslides		
slapstick	st ck			
sleepwalk	ee alk	sleepwalks	sleepwalked	sleepwalking
slowdown	ow	slowdowns		
slowpoke	ow o-e	slowpokes		

sm

/sm/ in smile

Position: Beginning

Vocalization: Voiced

Classification: Blend

Group: S-Blends

- **SM** is a blend. The **S** and **M** retain their original sounds.

Base	LT's	-s/-es	-ed	-ing	-y/-ly	-er	-est
smack	ck	smacks	smacked	smacking		smacker	
small	all					smaller	smallest
smart	ar	smarts	smarted	smarting	smartly	smarter	smartest
smash	sh	smashes	smashed	smashing		smasher	
smear	ear	smears	smeared	smearing			
smell	ll	smells	smelled	smelling	smelly	smellier	smelliest
smile	i-e	smiles	smiled	smiling	smiley	smiler	
smirk	ir	smirks	smirked	smirking	smirky	smirkier	smirkiest
smite	i-e	smites		smiting			
Smith	th	Smith's					
smock	ck	smocks	smocked	smocking			
smog					smoggy	smoggier	smoggiest
smoke	o-e	smokes	smoked	smoking	smoky	smoker	
smooch	oo ch	smooches	smooched	smooching			
smooth	oo th	smooths	smoothed	smoothing	smoothly	smoother	smoothest
smudge	dge	smudges	smudged	smudging	smudgy		

See next page for SM compound words.

Compound

blacksmith	bl ck th	blacksmiths
smokeless	o-e ss	
smokescreen	o-e scr ee	smokescreens
smokestack	o-e ck st	smokestacks
wordsmith	wor th	wordsmiths

sn

/sn/ in snack

Position: Beginning

Vocalization: Voiced

Classification: Blend

Group: S-Blends

- **SN** is a blend. The **S** and **N** retain their original sounds.

Base	LT's	-s/-es	-ed	-ing	-y/-ly	-er	-est
snack	ck	snacks	snacked	snacking		snacker	
snag		snags	snagged	snagging			
snail	ai	snails					
snake	a-e	snakes	snaked	snaking			
snap		snaps	snapped	snapping		snapper	
snare	are	snares	snared	snaring			
snatch	tch	snatches	snatched	snatching		snatcher	
sneak	ea	sneaks	sneaked	sneaking	sneaky	sneaker	
sneer	ee	sneers	sneered	sneering			
sneeze	ee ze	sneezes	sneezed	sneezing	sneezy	sneezer	
snide	i-e				snidely		
sniff	ff	sniffs	sniffed	sniffing	sniffy	sniffer	
snip		snips	snipped	snipping	snippy	*snippier*	*snippiest*
snipe	i-e	snipes	sniped	sniping		sniper	
snitch	tch	snitches	snitched	snitching			
snob		snobs			snobby	*snobbier*	*snobbiest*
snoop	oo	snoops	snooped	snooping		snooper	
snoot	oo				snooty	*snootier*	*snootiest*
snooze	oo ze	snoozes	snoozed	snoozing		snoozer	
snore	ore	snores	snored	snoring		snorer	
snort	or	snorts	snorted	snorting			
snot					snotty		

Base	LT's	-s/-es	-ed	-ing	-y/-ly	-er	-est
snout	ou	snouts					
snow	ow	snows	snowed	snowing	snowy	*snowier*	*snowiest*
snub		snubs	snubbed	snubbing			
snuck	ck						
snuff	ff	snuffs	snuffed	snuffing			
snug					snugly		

sp

/sp/ in space

Position: Beginning

Vocalization: Unvoiced

Classification: Blend

Group: S-Blends

- **SP** is a blend. The **S** and **P** retain their original sounds.
- **SP** is also an end blend. For words with **SP** at the end, see the End Blends section of this book.

Base	LT's	-s/-es	-ed	-ing	-y/-ly	-er	-est
spa		spas					
space	a-e c(e)	spaces	spaced	spacing	spacy	spacer	
spade	a-e	spades					
Spam							
span		spans	spanned	spanning		spanner	
spank	ank	spanks	spanked	spanking			
spar	ar	spars	sparred	sparring			
spare	are	spares	spared	sparing			
spark	ar	sparks	sparked	sparking	Sparky		
sparse	ar se				sparsely		
spat		spats				spatter	
spate	a-e						
spawn	aw	spawns	spawned	spawning			
spay	ay	spays	spayed	spaying			
speak	ea	speaks		speaking		speaker	
spear	ear	spears	speared	spearing			
speck	ck	specks					
sped							

Base	LT's	-s/-es	-ed	-ing	-y/-ly	-er	
speech	ee ch	speeches					
speed	ee	speeds		speeding	speedy	speeder	
spell	ll	spells	spelled	spelling		speller	
spend	nd	spends		spending		spender	
spent	nt						
spew	ew	spews	spewed	spewing			
spice	i-e c(e)	spices	spiced	spicing	spicy	*spicier*	*spiciest*
spike	i-e	spikes	spiked	spiking	spiky		
spill	ll	spills	spilled	spilling		spiller	
spin		spins		spinning	spinny	spinner	
spine	i-e	spines			spiny		
spire	ire	spires					
spit		spits		spitting		spitter	
spite	i-e	spites	spited	spiting			
split		splits		splitting		splitter	
spoil	oi	spoils	spoiled	spoiling		spoiler	
spoke	o-e						
sponge	o* g(e)	sponges	sponged	sponging	spongy	*spongier*	*spongiest*
spoof	oo	spoofs	spoofed	spoofing			
spook	oo	spooks	spooked	spooking	spooky	*spookier*	*spookiest*
spool	oo	spools	spooled	spooling			
spoon	oo	spoons	spooned	spooning			
spore	ore	spores					
sport	or	sports	sported	sporting	sporty	*sportier*	*sportiest*
spot		spots	spotted	spotting	spotty	*spottier*	*spottiest*
spout	ou	spouts	spouted	spouting			
spud		spuds					
spume	u-e	spumes					
spun							
spunk	unk				spunky	*spunkier*	*spunkiest*
spur	ur	spurs	spurred	spurring			
spurn	ur	spurns	spurned	spurning			
spurt	ur	spurts	spurted	spurting			
spy	y	spies	spied	spying			

Base	LT's	-s/-es	-ed	-ing	-y/-ly	-er	-est
airspace	air ace						
airspeed	air ee						
allspice	all ice						
cyberspace	c(y) er ace						
downspout	ow ou	downspouts					
godspeed	ee						
homespun	o-e						
hotspot		hotspots					
lifespan	i-e	lifespans					
nightspot	ight	nightspots					
spacecraft	ace cr ft	spacecrafts					
spaceman	ace						
spacemen	ace						
spaceship	ace sh	spaceships					
spacesuit	ace ui	spacesuits					
spacewalk	ace alk						
sparerib	are	spareribs					
spearhead	ear ea	spearheads					
speechless	ee ch ss				speechlessly		
speedway	ee ay	speedways					
spellbound	ll ou nd						
spiderweb	i-e er	spiderwebs					
spillover	ll er						
spitball	all	spitballs					
spoilsport	oi or	spoilsports					
spokesman	o-e -s						
sportscast	or -s st						
sportswear	or -s ear						
spotless	ss				spotlessly		
spotlight	ight	spotlights					
spymaster	y st er						
sunspot		sunspots					
tailspin	ai	tailspins					
teaspoon	ea oo	teaspoons					
wellspring	ll ing						
wingspan	ing	wingspans					

st

/st/ in stick

Position: Beginning and End

Vocalization: Unvoiced

Classification: Blend

Group: S-Blends

- **ST** is a blend. The **S** and **T** retain their original sounds.
- **ST** is also an end blend. For words with **ST** at the end, see the End Blends section of this book.

Base	LT's	-s/-es	-ed	-ing	-y/-ly	-er	-est
stab		stabs	stabbed	stabbing			
stack	ck	stacks	stacked	stacking		stacker	
staff	ff	staffs	staffed	staffing		staffer	
stage	a-e g(e)	stages	staged	staging	stagy	stager	
stain	ai	stains	stained	staining			
stake	a-e	stakes	staked	staking			
stale	a-e					staler	stalest
stalk	alk	stalks	stalked	stalking		stalker	
stamp	mp	stamps	stamped	stamping		stamper	
stand	nd	stands		standing		stander	
stank	ank						
stare	a-e	stares	stared	staring			
stark	ar				starkly		
star	ar	stars	starred	starring	starry	starrier	starriest
stash	sh	stashes	stashed	stashing			
state	a-e	states	stated	stating	stately		
stave	a-e	staves	staved	staving			
stay	ay	stays	stayed	staying		stayer	
steak	ea	steaks					
steal	ea	steals		stealing		stealer	
steam	ea	steams	steamed	steaming	steamy	steamer	

Base	LT's	-s/-es/'s	-ed	-ing	-y/-ly	-er	-est
steed	ee	steeds					
steel	ee	steels	steeled	steeling		Steeler	
steep	ee	steeps	steeped	steeping	steeply	steeper	steepest
steer	eer	steers	steered	steering			
stem		stems	stemmed	stemming			
step		steps	stepped	stepping		stepper	
stern	er				sternly		
stew	ew	stews	stewed	stewing			
stick	ck	sticks		sticking		sticker	
stiff	ff	stiffs	stiffed	stiffing	stiffly		
stile	i-e	stiles					
still	ll	stills	stilled	stilling		stiller	stillest
stilt	lt	stilts	stilted	stilting			
sting	ing	stings		stinging		stinger	
stink	ink	stinks		stinking	stinky	stinker	
stint	nt	stints	stinted	stinting			
stir	ir	stirs	stirred	stirring		stirrer	
stock	ck	stocks	stocked	stocking		stocker	
stoke	o-e	stokes	stoked	stoking			
stole	o-e						
stomp	mp	stomps	stomped	stomping		stomper	
stone	o-e	stones	stoned	stoning			
stood	oo						
stool	oo	stools					
stoop	oo	stoops	stooped	stooping			
stop		stops	stopped	stopping		stopper	
store	o-e	stores	stored	storing	story		
story	o-e y	stories					
stork	or	storks					
storm	or	storms	stormed	storming	stormy	stormier	stormiest
stout	ou				stoutly	stouter	stoutest
stove	o-e	stoves					
stow	ow	stows	stowed	stowing			
stub		stubs	stubbed	stubbing			
stuck	ck						
stud		studs	studded	studding			
stump	mp	stumps	stumped	stumping		stumper	
stun		stuns	stunned	stunning		stunner	
stung	ung						
stunt	nt	stunts	stunted	stunting			
sty	y	sties					
style	y-e	styles	styled	styling			

Base	LT's	-s/-es	-ed	-ing	-y/-ly	-er	-est
backstage	ck age						
backstop	ck	backstops					
bandstand	nd	bandstands					
barnstorm	ar or	barnstorms	barnstormed	barnstorming			
bedstead	ea	bedsteads					
beefsteak	ee ea	beefsteaks					
bookstore	oo ore	bookstores					
brainstorm	br ai or	brainstorms					
broomstick	br oo ck	broomsticks					
brownstone	br ow o-e						
cornstarch	or ar ch						
dipstick	ck	dipsticks					
doorstep	oor	doorsteps					
doorstop	oor	doorstops					
downstage	ow age						
downstairs	ow air -s						
drugstore	dr ore	drugstores					
drumstick	dr ck	drumsticks					
drumstick	dr ck	drumsticks					
farmstead	ar ea	farmsteads					
firestorm	ire or	firestorms					
Flagstaff	fl ff						
foodstuff	oo ff						
footstep	oo						
footstep	oo	footsteps					
footstool	oo	footstools					
footstool	oo	footstools					
forecast	ore	forecasts					
freestyle	fr ee y-e						
frostbite	fr i-e						
gallstone	all o-e	gallstones					
grandstand	gr nd	grandstand		grandstanding			
gravestone	gr a-e o-e	gravestones					
hailstone	ai o-e	hailstones					
hailstorm	ai or	hailstorms					
hairstyle	air y-e	hairstyles					
hatstand	nd	hatstands					
haystack	ay ck	haystacks					
homestead	o-e ea	homesteads					
inkstand	ink nd	inkstands					
joystick	oy ck	joysticks					

lifestyle	i-e y-e	lifestyles		
lipstick	ck	lipsticks		
livestock	i-e ck			
lodestone	o-e	lodestones		
mainstay	ai ay			
newsstand	ew nd	newsstands		
nightstick	ight ck	nightsticks		
offstage	ff age			
onstage	age			
sandstone	nd o-e			
sandstorm	nd or	sandstorms		
snowstorm	ow or	snowstorms		
soapstone	oa o-e			
stagehand	age nd	stageshands		
stainless	ai ss			
staircase	air a-e	staircases		
stairway	air ay	stairways		
stairwell	air ll	stairwells		
stakeout	a-e ou	stakeout		
stakeout	a-e ou	stakeouts		
stalemate	a-e	stalemates		
standby	nd y			
standby	nd y			
standoff	nd ff			
standoff	nd ff	standoffs		
standout	nd ou			
standup	nd			
starboard	ar oar			
stardom	ar			
stardust	ar			
starfish	ar sh	starfishes		
starfruit	ar fr ui			
starless	ar ss			
starlight	ar ight			
starlit	ar			
statehood	a-e oo			
stateroom	a-e oo			
stateside	a-e i-e			
statesmen	a-e -s			
statewide	a-e i-e			
steamboat	ea oa	steamboats		
steamship	ea sh	steamships		
stockpile	ck i-e	stockpiles	stockpiled	stockpiling

stockroom	ck oo	stockrooms		
stockyard	ck ar	stockyards		
stonewall	o-e all	stonewalls	stonewalled	stonewalling
stoneware	o-e are			
stonework	o-e wor			
stopgap				
stoplight	ight	stoplights		
stopwatch	wa tch	stopwatches		
storefront	o* ore fr nt	storefronts		
storehouse	ore ou -se	storehouses		
storeroom	ore oo	storerooms		
sweepstake	sw ee a-e			
toadstool	oa oo	toadstools		
tombstone	mb o-e	tombstones		
typecast	y-e	typecasts		typecasting
upstage	age	upstages	upstaged	upstaging
upstart	ar	upstarts		
washstand	wa sh nd			
withstand	th nd	withstands		withstanding
withstood	th oo			
yardstick	ar ck	yardsticks		

SW

/sw/ in swing

Position: Beginning

Vocalization: Voiced

Classification: Blend

Group: S-Blend

- **SW** is a blend. **S** and **W** retain their original sounds.
- Some **SW** words are followed by an **/ah/** sound for the **a**, as in **swan** or **swap**.

Base	LT's	-s/-es	-ed	-ing	-y/-ly	-er	-est
swag		swags				swagger	
swain	ai	swains					
swam							
swamp	wa mp	swamps	swamped	swamping	swampy	swampier	swampiest
swan	wa	swans					
swank	ank						
swap	wa	swaps	swapped	swapping		swapper	
swat	wa	swats	swatted	swatting		swatter	
sway	ay	sways	swayed	swaying			
swear	ear	swears		swearing			
sweat	ea	sweats	sweated	sweating	sweaty	sweatier	sweatiest
Swede	e-e	Swedes					
sweep	ee	sweeps		sweeping		sweeper	
sweet	ee	sweets			sweetly	sweeter	sweetest
swell	ll	swells	swelled	swelling			
swept	pt						
swerve	er ve	swerves	swerved	swerving			
swift	ft				swiftly	swifter	swiftest
swig		swigs	swigged	swigging			

Base	LT's	-s/-es/'s	-ed	-ing	-y/-ly	-er	-est
swill	ll	swills	swilled	swilling			
swim		swims		swimming	Swimmy	swimmer	
swine	i-e						
swing	ing	swings		swinging			
swipe	i-e	swipes	swiped	swiping		swiper	
swirl	ir	swirls	swirled	swirling	swirly		
swish	sh	swishes	swished	swishing	swishy		
switch	tch	switches	switched	switching		switcher	
swoon	oo	swoons	swooned	swooning			
sword	w*	swords					
swore	ore						
sworn	or						
swung	ung						

R-blends– Printable Cards

br

cr

dr

fr

gr	pr
tr	

br

/br/ in brick

Position: Beginning

Vocalization: Voiced

Classification: Blend

Group: R-Blends

- **BR** is a blend.. The **B** and **R** retain their original sounds.

Base		-s/-es/'s	-ed	-ing	-y/-ly	-er	-est
brace	a-e c(e)	braces	braced	bracing		bracer	
Brad		Brad's					
brag		brags	bragged	bragging		bragger	
braid	ai	braids	braided	braiding		braider	
brain	ai	brains			brainy		
brake	a-e	brakes	braked	braking			
Bram		Bram's					
bran							
brand	nd	brands	branded	branding			
brash	sh				brashly	brasher	brashest
brass	ss	brasses			brassy		
brave	a-e	braves	braved	braving	bravely	braver	bravest
bread	ea	breads	breaded	breading			
break	ea	breaks		breaking		breaker	
breed	ee	breeds				breeder	
bribe	i-e	bribes	bribed	bribing			
brick	ck	bricks	bricked	bricking			
bride	i-e	brides					
brief	ie	briefs	briefed	briefing	briefly	briefer	briefest
brim		brims	brimmed	brimming			
brine	i-e	brines	brined	brining			
bring	ing	brings		bringing		bringer	

Base	LT's	-s/-es/'s	-ed	-ing	-y/-ly	-er	-est
brink	ink						
brisk	sk				briskly	brisker	briskest
broad	oa				broadly	broader	broadest
broil	oi	broils	broiled	broiling		broiler	
broke	o-e					broker	
brook	oo	brooks					
broom	oo	brooms					
broth	th						
brow	ow	brows					
brown	ow	browns	browned	browning		browner	brownest
brush	sh	brushes	brushed	brushing		brusher	
brute	u-e	brutes					
Bryce	y c(e)	Bryce's					

Compound

Base	LT's	-s/-es	-ed	-ing	-ly
birdbrain	ir ai	birdbrains			
bracelet	ace	bracelets			
brainchild	ai ch ild				
brainless	ai ss				brainlessly
brainstorm	ai st or	brainstorms			
brainwash	ai wa sh	brainwashes	brainwashed	brainwashing	
brainwave	ai a-e	brainwaves			
breadbasket	ea sk	breadbaskets			
breadboard	ea oar	breadboards			
breadcrumb	ea cr mb	breadcrumbs			
breadline	ea i-e	breadlines			
breakdown	ea ow				
breakfast	ea st	breakfasts	breakfasted	breakfasting	
breakneck	ea -ck				
breakup	ea	breakups			
breathless	ea th ss				breathlessly
brickwork	-ck wor	brickworks			
bridegroom	i-e gr oo	bridegrooms			
bridesmaid	i-e ai	bridesmaids			
briefcase	ie a-e	briefcases			
brimstone	st o-e				

Base	LT's	-s/-es	-ed	-ing	-y/-ly	-er	-est
broadcast	oa st	broadcasts					
broadside	oa i-e						
broomstick	oo st ck	broomsticks					
browbeat	ow ea	browbeats					
brownstone	ow st o-e	brownstones					
brushstroke	sh str o-e	brushstrokes					
brushwood	sh oo						
brushwork	sh wor						
daybreak	ay ea						
firebrand	i-e nd	firebrands					
firebreak	i-e ea	firebreaks					
footbridge	oo dge	footbridges					
hairbrush	air sh	hairbrushes					
handbrake	nd a-e	handbrakes					
heartbreak	ear* ea	heartbreaks					
highbrow	igh ow						
jailbreak	ai ea	jailbreaks					
lowbrow	ow						
outbreak	ou ea	outbreaks					
shortbread	sh or ea						
sweetbread	sw ee ea						
toothbrush	oo th sh	toothbrushes					
underbrush	er sh						
windbreak	nd ea					windbreaker	

<u>cr</u>

/cr/ in crab

Position: Beginning

Vocalization: Voiced

Classification: Blend

Group: R-Blends

- **CR** is a blend. The **C** and **R** retain their original sounds.

Base		-s/-es/'s	-ed	-ing	-y/-ly	-er	-est
crab		crabs	crabbed	crabbing	crabby	*crabbier*	*crabbiest*
craft	ft	crafts	crafted	crafting	crafty	crafter	
Craig	ai	Craig's					
cram		crams	crammed	cramming		crammer	
cramp	mp	cramps	cramped	cramping			
crane	a-e	cranes	craned	craning			
crank	ank	cranks	cranked	cranking	cranky		
crash	sh	crashes	crashed	crashing			
crate	a-e	crates	crated	crating		crater	
crave	a-e	craves	craved	craving			
creak	ea	creaks	creaked	creaking	creaky	*creakier*	*creakiest*
cream	ea	creams	creamed	creaming	creamy	creamer	
creed	ee	creeds					
creek	ee	creeks					
creep	ee	creeps	creeped	creeping	creepy	*creepier*	*creepiest*
crew	ew	crews	crewed	crewing			
crib		cribs					
crime	i-e	crimes					
croak	oa	croaks	croaked	croaking			
crock	ck	crocks					
crook	oo	crooks					
croon	oo	croons	crooned	crooning		crooner	

Base	LT's	-s/-es/'s	-ed	-ing	-y/-ly	-er	-est
crop		crops	cropped	cropping		cropper	
cross	ss	crosses	crossed	crossing		crosser	crossest
crow	ow	crows	crowed	crowing			
crowd	ow	crowds	crowded	crowding			
crown	ow	crowns	crowned	crowning			
crude	u-e				crudely	cruder	crudest
crumb	mb	crumbs					
crush	sh	crushes	crushed	crushing		crusher	
crust	st	crusts	crusted	crusting	crusty		

Compound

Base	LT's	-s/-es	-ed	-ing	-y/-ly
aircraft	ai ft	aircrafts			
breadcrumb	br ea mb	breadcrumbs			
crabgrass	gr ss				
crankshaft	ank sh ft	crankshafts			
crawfish	aw sh	crawfishes			
crossbar	ss ar	crossbars			
crossbow	ss ow	crossbows			
crossbreed	ss br ee	crossbreeds			
crosscheck	ss ch ck	crosschecks			
crossfire	ss ire				
crosstown	ss ow				
crosswalk	ss alk	crosswalks			
outcrop	ou	outcrops	outcropped	outcropping	
scarecrow	sc are ow	scarecrows			

dr

/dr/ in drive

Position: Beginning

Vocalization: Voiced

Classification: Blend

Group: R-Blends

- **DR** is a blend. The **D** and **R** retain their original sounds.
- Some students will hear or pronounce the beginning sound of **DR** words as **/JR/** (**drive, drain**).

Base		-s/-es	-ed	-ing	-y/-ly	-er	-est
drab							drabbest
draft	ft	drafts	drafted	drafting	drafty	draftier	draftiest
drag		drags	dragged	dragging		dragger	
drain	ai	drains	drained	draining		drainer	
Drake	a-e	Drake's					
drank	ank						
drape	a-e	drapes	draped	draping		draper	
draw	aw	draws		drawing		drawer	
drawl	aw	drawls	drawled	drawling			
dread	ea	dreads	dreaded	dreading			
dream	ea	dreams	dreamed	dreaming	dreamy	dreamer	
dress	ss	dresses	dressed	dressing	dressy	dresser	
drew	ew						
Drew	ew	Drew's					
drift	ft	drifts	drifted	drifting		drifter	
drill	ll	drills	drilled	drilling		driller	
drink	ink	drinks		drinking		drinker	
drip		drips	dripped	dripping	drippy	dripper	
drive	i-e	drives		driving		driver	
drone	o-e	drones	droned	droning			

Base		-s/-es	-ed	-ing	-y/-ly	-er	-est
drool	oo	drools	drooled	drooling		drooler	
drop		drops	dropped	dropping		dropper	
drove	o-e						
drown	ow	drowns	drowned	drowning			
drug		drugs	drugged	drugging			
drum		drums	drummed	drumming		drummer	

Compound

Base	LT's	-s/-es	-ed	-ing	-y/-ly	-er	-est
backdrop	ck	backdrops					
dragnet		dragnets					
dragonfly	fl y	dragonflies					
drainpipe	ai i-e	drainpipes					
drawback	aw ck	drawbacks					
driveway	i-e ay	driveways					
dropout	ou	dropouts					
drumbeat	ea	drumbeats					
drumstick	st ck	drumsticks					
eardrum	ear	eardrums					
eavesdrop	ea -es	eavesdrops					
hairdryer	air y -er	hairdryers					
overdraw	er aw	overdraws		overdrawing			
raindrop	ai	raindrops					
sundress	ss	sundresses					
teardrop	ear	teardrops					
withdraw	th aw	withdraws		withdrawing			
withdrew	th ew						

fr

/fr/ in free

Position: Beginning

Vocalization: Voiced

Classification: Blend

Group: R-Blends

- **FR** is a blend. The **F** and **R** retain their original sounds.

Base	PG	-s/-es/'s	-ed	-ing	-y/-ly	-er	-est
frail	ai					frailer	frailest
frame	a-e	frames	framed	framing		framer	
Fran		Fran's					
frank	ank				frankly	franker	frankest
Frank	ank	Frank's					
fraud	au						
freak	ea	freaks	freaked	freaking	freaky		
Fred		Fred's					
free	ee	frees	freed	freeing	freely	freer	freest
freed	ee						
freeze	ee ze	freezes		freezing		freezer	
fresh	sh				freshly	fresher	freshest
frill	ll	frills	frilled	frilling	frilly		
frisk	sk	frisks	frisked	frisking	frisky	friskier	friskiest
Fritz	tz	Fritz's					
frizz	zz	frizzes	frizzed	frizzing	frizzy		
frock	ck	frocks					
frog		frogs			froggy	frogger	
frost	st	frosts	frosted	frosting	frosty	frostier	frostiest
froth	th						
frown	ow	frowns	frowned	frowning			
froze	o-e						
fruit	ui	fruits			fruity	fruitier	fruitiest

Compound

Base	LT's	-s/-es	-ed	-ing	-y/-ly	-er	-est
bullfrog	u ll -s	bullfrogs					
carefree	are ee						
framework	a-e wor	frameworks					
freeload	ee oa	freeloads					
freestyle	ee st y -le	freestyles	freestyled	freestyling			
freeware	ee are						
freshman	sh						
freshwater	sh wa -er						
friendless	ie nd ss						
friendship	ie nd sh	friendships					
frostbite	st i-e						
fruitcake	ui a-e	fruitcakes					
girlfriend	ie ir nd	girlfriends					
grapefruit	gr a-e ui	grapefruits					
mainframe	ai a-e	mainframes					
proofread	oo ea	proofreads					
starfruit	st ar ui	starfruits					
upfront	*o nt						

gr

/gr/ in grass

Position: Beginning

Vocalization: Voiced

Classification: Blend

Group: R-Blends

- **GR** is a blend. The **G** and **R** retain their original sounds.

Base	-s/-es/'s	-ed	-ing	-y/-ly	-er	-est
grab		grabs	grabbed	grabbing	grabby	grabber	
Grace	c(e) a-e	Grace's					
grace	c(e) a-e	graces					
grade	a-e	grades	graded	grading		grader	
graft	ft	grafts	grafted	grafting		grafter	
Graham	h*	Graham's					
grail	ai						
grain	ai	grains			grainy		
grand	nd					grander	grandest
grant	nt	grants	granted	granting		granter	
Grant		Grant's					
grape	a-e	grapes					
graph	ph	graphs	graphed	graphing			
grasp	sp	grasps	grasped	grasping		grasper	
grass	ss	grasses			grassy	*grassier*	*grassiest*
grate	a-e	grates	grated	grating		grater	
grave	a-e	graves			gravy	graver	gravest
great	ea	greats			greatly	greater	greatest
greed	ee				greedy	*greedier*	*greediest*
green	ee					greener	greenest
Greer	eer	Greer's					
greet	ee	greets	greeted	greeting		greeter	

Base	LT's	-s/-es/'s	-ed	-ing	-y/-ly	-er	-est
grew	ew						
Grey	ey	Grey's					
grid		grids	gridded	gridding		gridder	
grief	ie						
grill	ll	grills	grilled	grilling		griller	
grim					grimly	grimmer	grimmest
grime	i-e				grimy		
grin		grins	grinned	grinning		grinner	
grind	ind	grinds		grinding		grinder	
grip		grips	gripped	gripping		gripper	
grit		grits	gritted	gritting	gritty	grittier	grittiest
groin	oi						
groom	oo	grooms	groomed	grooming		groomer	
gross	ss				grossly	grosser	grossest
group	ou	groups	grouped	grouping		grouper	
grout	ou					grouter	
grove	o-e	groves				Grover	
grow	ow	grows		growing		grower	
growl	ow	growls	growled	growling	growly	growler	
grown	ow						
grub		grubs					
gruff	ff				gruffly	gruffer	gruffest
grump	mp	grumps	grumped	grumping	grumpy	grumpier	grumpiest
grunt	nt	grunts	grunted	grunting		grunter	

See next page for GR compound words.

Compound

Base	LT's	-s/-es	-ed	-ing	-y/-ly -er -est
background	ck ou nd	backgrounds			
bluegrass	bl ue ss				
bridegroom	br i-e oo	bridegrooms			
campground	mp ou nd	campgrounds			
crabgrass	cr ss				
downgrade	ow a-e	downgrades	downgraded	downgrading	
evergreen	er ee				
grandchild	nd ch ld				
granddaughter	nd aught -er				
grandma	nd	grandmas			
grandpa	nd	grandpas			
grandson	nd	grandsons			
grandstand	nd st	grandstands			
grapefruit	a-e fr ui	grapefruits			
grapevine	a-e i-e	grapevines			
grassland	ss nd	grasslands			
gravestone	a-e st o-e	gravestones			
graveyard	a-e ar	graveyards			
greenback	ee ck	greenbacks			
greenhorn	ee or	greenhorns			
greenhouse	ee ou se	greenhouses			
greyhound	ey ou nd	greyhounds			
grindstone	ind st o-e	grindstones			
groomsmen	oo -s				
groundcloth	ou nd cl th	groundcloths			
groundhog	ou nd	groundhogs			
ingrown	ow				
newsgroup	ew ou -s	newgroups			
outgrew	ou ew				
outgrow	ou ow	outgrows		outgrowing	
playground	pl ay ou nd	playgrounds			
playgroup	pl ay ou	playgroups			
showground	sh ow ou nd	showgrounds			
showroom	sh ow oo	showrooms			
upgrade	a-e	upgrades	upgraded	upgrading	
wholegrain	wh o-e ai				

pr

/pr/ in pray

Position: Beginning

Vocalization: Voiced

Classification: Blend

Group: R-Blends

- **PR** is a blend. The **P** and **R** retain their original sounds.

Base		-s/-es	-ed	-ing	-y/-ly	-er	-est
praise	ai se	praises	praised	praising			
prance	ce	prances	pranced	prancing		Prancer	
prank	ank	pranks	pranked	pranking			
pray	ay	prays	prayed	praying		prayer	
preen	ee	preens	preened	preening			
prep		preps	prepped	prepping	preppy	prepper	
price	i-e ce	prices	priced	pricing	pricy	*pricier*	*priciest*
Price	ice	Price's					
prick	ck	pricks	pricked	pricking	prickly	pricker	
pride	i-e						
prim					primly		
prime	i-e	primes	primed	priming		primer	
primp	mp	primps	primped	primping			
Prince	c(e)	Prince's					
print	nt	prints	printed	printing		printer	
prize	i-e	prizes	prized	prizing			
probe	o-e	probes	probed	probing		prober	
prom		proms					
prone	o-e						
proof	oo	proofs	proofed	proofing		proofer	
proud	ou				proudly	prouder	proudest
prove	ove*	proves	proved	proving			

prowl	ow	prowls	prowled	prowling	prowler
prune	u-e	prunes	pruned	pruning	pruner
pry	y	pries	pried	prying	

Compound

Base	LT's	-s/-es/'s	-ed	-ing	-y/-ly	-er	-est
fireproof	ire oo						
foolproof	oo						
footprint	oo nt	footprints					
footprint	nt	footprints					
heatproof	ea oo						
newsprint	ew nt -s						
pinprick	ck	pinpricks					
pratfall	all						
priceless	i-e ice ss						
prizefight	i-e ight						
proofread	oo ea	proofreads		proofreading		proofreader	
waterproof	wa er oo						

tr

/tr/ in train

Position: Beginning

Vocalization: Voiced

Classification: Blend

Group: T-Blends or R-Blends

- **TR** is a blend. **The T** and **R** both retain their original sounds.
- Some students will hear or pronounce **/ch/** at the beginning of **TR** words, such as **train** and **track**.

Base		-s/-es/'s	-ed	-ing	-y/-ly	-er/-or	-est
trace	a-e ace	traces	traced	tracing		tracer	
track	ck	tracks	tracked	tracking		tracker	
tract	ct	tracts					
trade	a-e	trades	traded	trading		trader	
trail	ai	trails	trailed	trailing		trailer	
train	ai	trains	trained	training		trainer	
trait	ai	traits				traitor	
tramp	mp	tramps	tramped	tramping			
trance	c(e)	trances					
trap		traps	trapped	trapping		trapper	
trash	sh	trashes	trashed	trashing	trashy	trashier	trashiest
tray	ay	trays					
tread	ea	treads	treaded	treading			
treat	ea	treats	treated	treating			
tree	ee	trees	treed	treeing			
trend	nd	trends	trended	trending	trendy	trendier	trendiest
Trent	nt	Trent's					
tribe	i-e	tribes					

Base		-s/-es/'s	-ed	-ing	-y/-ly	-er/-or	-est
trick	ck	tricks	tricked	tricking	tricky	*trickier*	*trickiest*
trike	i-e	trikes					
trim		trims	trimmed	trimming		trimmer	
trip		trips	tripped	tripping			
trite	i-e				tritely		
troll	oll	trolls	trolled	trolling			
tromp	mp	tromps	tromped	tromping			
troop	oo	troops	trooped	trooping		trooper	
trot		trots	trotted	trotting		trotter	
trout	ou						
Troy	oy	Troy's					
truce	u-e c(e)	truces					
truck	ck	trucks	trucked	trucking		trucker	
true	ue				truly	truer	truest
trunk	unk	trunks					
trust	st	trusts	trusted	trusting			
truth	u th	truths					
try	y	tries	tried	trying			

See next page for **TR** compound words.

Compound

Base	LT's	-s/-es	-ed	-ing
backtrack	ck	backtracks	backtracked	backtracking
foxtrot		foxtrots	foxtrotted	foxtrotting
racetrack	ace ck	racetracks		
shoetree	sh oe* ee	shoetrees		
sidetrack	i-e ck	sidetracks		
trackball	ck all	trackballs		
tracksuit	ck ui	tracksuits		
trademark	a-e ar	trademarks		
tradesmen	a-e -s			
tramway	ay	tramways		
trashcan	sh	trashcans		
treadmill	ea ll	treadmills		
treeline	ee i-e	treelines		
treetop	ee	treetops		
tryout	y ou	tryouts		

W Blends– Printable Cards

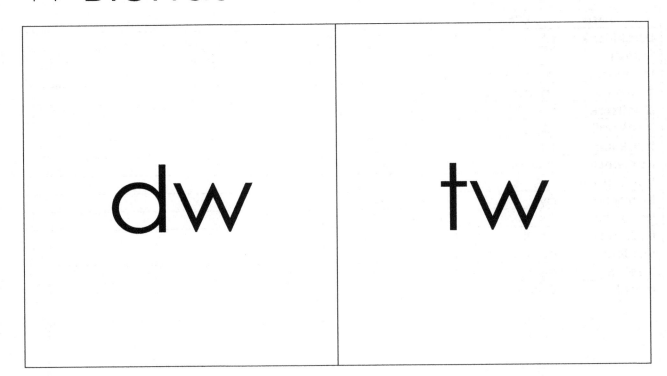

/dw/ in dwell

Position: Beginning

Vocalization: Voiced

Classification: Blend

Group: W-blends

- **DW** is a blend. The **D** and **W** retain their original sounds.
- Not all educators teach the **DW** blend, since it is so rare.

Base	PG	-s/-es	-ed	-ing	-y/-ly	-er	-est
dwarf	ar	dwarves	dwarfed	dwarfing			
dweeb	ee	dweebs					
dwell	ll	dwells	dwelled*	dwelling		dweller	
dwelt	lt						

Multisyllable

Base	PG	-s/-es	-ed	-ing	-y/-ly	-er	-est
dwindle	dle	dwindles	dwindled	dwindling			

*The past tense of **dwell** is **dwelt**, but in the US, sometimes **dwelled** is used.

tw

/tw/ in twin

Position: Beginning

Vocalization: Voiced

Classification: Blend

Group: W-Blends

- **TW** is a blend. The **T** and **W** both retain their original sounds.

Base	LT's	-s/-es	-ed	-ing	-y/-ly	-er	-est
twang	ang	twangs	twanged	twanging			
tweak	ea	tweaks	tweaked	tweaking			
tweed	ee	tweeds			tweedy	*tweedier*	*tweediest*
tweet	ee	tweets	tweeted	tweeting		tweeter	
twelfth	lf th						
twelve	ve						
twice	i-e c(e)						
twig		twigs					
twill	ll	twills	twilled	twilling			
twin		twins	twinned	twinning			
twine	i-e	twines	twined	twining			
twirl	ir	twirls	twirled	twirling	twirly		
twist	st	twists	twisted	twisting	twisty	twister	
twitch	tch	twitches	twitched	twitching	twitchy		

End Blends– Printable Cards

Two different word family lists are provided, one with short vowels only (in black ink), and the other with alternative vowel sounds (in grey ink). Some end blend word families (such as OST) have both a short vowel sound and a long vowel sound (cost, post). Those are listed twice, both in black ink and in grey ink. Combinations with vowel teams are not included, because vowel teams are generally taught after end blends. Vowel teams lists can be found in Volume 2.

ck	**ack** **eck** **ick** **ock** **uck**

ct	act
	ect
	ict
	oct
	uct

ft	aft
	eft
	ift
	oft
	uft

ld	eld	ald ild old

| lf | elf
ilf
olf
ulf | alf |

lk	elk ilk ulk	alk olk

lp	alp elp ulp

lt

elt
ilt
ult

alt
olt

mp

amp
emp
imp
omp
ump

nd	and end ind ond und	ind

nt	ant ent int ont unt

pt	apt ept ipt opt upt
sk	ask esk isk osk usk

sp

asp
isp
usp

st

ast
est
ist
ost
ust

ost

tz

etz
itz
utz

ck

/k/ in duck

Position: End

Vocalization: Unvoiced

Classification: Blend

Group: End Blend, Short Soldier

- **-CK** is found at the end of a one-syllable base word and only follows a short vowel sound.
- As a rule, words do not end in just **C** or **K**. However, there are many ways to spell the **/k/** sound at the end of a word. **-CK** is used for short vowel one-syllable words. A word can end with the suffix **-IC**. Words with **VCE** patterns can end with **-KE** (bike). Multi-syllable words can end in **-QUE** (unique).
- **-CK** prevents the **C** from saying its soft sound when a vowel suffix is added at the end of a word. (**pricking** vs. **pricing**).
- **CK** functions as a double **K** in many situations. For example, in the word **baking**, the **A** is long, because there is only one consonant following it. For the word **backing**, the **A** is short because it is followed by two consonants. This is a similar function to why we double the letter in many words. In the word **dinner**, the **N** is doubled to keep the **I** short. In the word **diner**, there is only one **N**, so the **I** is long.
- A **K** is sometimes added to a **C** when a vowel suffix is added to the end of a word that ends in **C**, to prevent the **C** from saying its short sound. For example, **panic** becomes **panicking**.
- **CK** is one of the few end blends that can be easily taught in isolation, because it is easy to pronounce. The word families for **CK** are **ack, eck, ick, ock, uck**.

ck

Base		-s/-es	-ed	-ing	-y/-ly	-er	-est
back		backs	backed	backing		backer	
beck							
black	bl					blacker	blackest
block	bl	blocks	blocked	blocking		blocker	
brick	br	bricks	bricked	bricking		bricker	
buck		bucks	bucked	bucking			
check	ch	checks	checked	checking		checker	
chick	ch	chicks					
chock	ch						
chuck	ch	chucks	chucked	chucking		chucker	
Chuck	ch	Chuck's			Chucky		
clack	cl	clacks	clacked	clacking		clacker	
click	cl	clicks	clicked	clicking		clicker	
clock	cl	clocks	clocked	clocking			
cluck	cl	clucks	clucked	clucking	clucky	clucker	
crack	cr	cracks	cracked	cracking		cracker	
crick	cr						
crock	cr	crocks				Crocker	
deck		decks	decked	decking		decker	
Dick		Dick's					
dock		docks	docked	docking		docker	
duck		ducks	ducked	ducking	ducky	ducker	
flack	fl						
fleck	fl	flecks	flecked	flecking			
flick	fl	flicks	flicked	flicking		flicker	
flock	fl	flocks	flocked	flocking			
frock	fr	frocks					
hack		hacks	hacked	hacking		hacker	
hock		hocks	hocked	hocking			
ick					icky		
Jack		Jack's			Jacky		
kick		kicks	kicked	kicking	kicky	kicker	
knack	kn						
knock	kn	knocks	knocked	knocking		knocker	
lack		lacks					
lick		licks	licked	licking		licker	
lock		locks	locked	locking		locker	
luck					lucky		

149

Base		-s/-es	-ed	-ing	-y/-ly/-ey	-er	-est
Mick		Mick's			Mickey		
mock		mocks	mocked	mocking		mocker	
muck					mucky		
neck		necks					
Nick		Nick's			Nicky		
pack		packs	packed	packing		packer	
peck		pecks	pecked	pecking			
pick		picks	picked	picking	picky	picker	
pluck	pl	plucks	plucked	plucking	plucky		
prick	pr	pricks	pricked	pricking	prickly	pricker	
puck		pucks				pucker	
quack	qu	quacks	quacked	quacking		quacker	
quick	qu				quickly	quicker	quickest
rack		racks	racked	racking			
Rick		Rick's			Ricky		
rock		rocks	rocked	rocking	Rocky	rocker	
sack		sacks	sacked	sacking			
shack	sh	shacks					
shock	sh	shocks	shocked	shocking		shocker	
shuck	sh	shucks	shucked	shucking		shucker	
sick					sickly	sicker	sickest
slack	sl	slacks	slacked	slacking		slacker	
slick	sl				slickly	slicker	slickest
smack	sm	smacks	smacked	smacking		smacker	
smock	sm	smocks	smocked	smocking			
snack	sn	snacks	snacked	snacking		snacker	
snuck	sn						
sock		socks	socked	socking			
stack	st	stacks	stacked	stacking		stacker	
stick	st	sticks		sticking	sticky	sticker	
stuck	st						
suck		sucks	sucked	sucking	sucky	sucker	
tack		tacks	tacked	tacking	tacky		
thick	th				thickly	thicker	
tick		ticks	ticked	ticking		ticker	
trick	tr	tricks	tricked	tricking	tricky		
tuck		tucks	tucked	tucking		Tucker	
whack	wh	whacks	whacked	whacking			
wick		wicks	wicked	wicking		wicker	
wreck	wr	wrecks	wrecked	wrecking		wrecker	
yack		yacks	yacked	yacking			

Base	LT's	-s/-es	-ed	-ing	-y/-ly	-er	-est
yuck					yucky		
Zack	Zack's						

Compound

Base	LT's	-s/-es	-ed	-ing	-y/-ly	-er	-est
backpack		backpacks					
backroom	oo						
backside	i-e	backsides					
backslide	i-e sl	backslides					
backstage	a-e st age						
backtrack	tr ck	backtracks					
backup							
backyard	ar	backyards					
bareback	a-e						
blackbird	bl ir	blackbirds					
blackjack	bl						
blacklist	bl st	blacklists					
blackmail	bl ai	blackmails					
blackout	bl ou	blackouts					
breakneck	br ea						
broomstick	br oo st	broomsticks					
carjack	ar	carjacks					
carsick	ar						
checkbook	ch oo	checkbooks					
checklist	ch st	checklists					
checkmate	ck a-e	checkmates					
checkout	ch ou	checkouts					
checkpoint	ch oi nt	checkpoints					
checkup	ch	checkups					
chickpea	ch ea	chickpeas					
chopstick	ch st	chopsticks					
clockwork	cl wor						
cockpit		cockpits					
cockroach	oa ch	cockroaches					
comeback	o-e*	comebacks					
crackdown	cr ow	crackdowns					
crosscheck	cr ss ch	crosschecks	crosschecked	crosschecking			
cutback		cutbacks					
deckhand	nd	deckhands					

Base	LT's	-s/-es	-ed	-ing	-y/-ly	-er	-est
dipstick	st	dipsticks					
dockside	i-e						
dockyard	ar	dockyards					
drawback	dr aw	drawbacks					
drumstick	dr st	drumsticks					
feedback	ee						
firebrick	ire br	firebricks					
flapjack	fl	flapjacks					
flashback	fl sh	flashbacks					
fullback	u ll	fullbacks					
greenback	gr ee	greenbacks					
hacksaw	aw	hacksaws					
halfback	alf	halfbacks					
hatchback	tch	hatchbacks					
haystack	st ay	haystacks					
homesick	o-e						
horseback	or se						
hunchback	nch						
jackpot		jackpots					
kickoff	ff	kickoffs					
knapsack	kn	knapsacks					
knickknack	kn	knickknacks					
knockoff	kn ff	knockoffs					
lipstick	st	lipsticks					
lockjaw	aw						
locksmith	sm th	locksmiths					
lockup		lockups					
matchstick	tch st	matchsticks					
moonstruck	oo str						
neckline	i-e	necklines					
necktie	ie	neckties					
nickname	a-e	nicknames					
nitpick		nitpicks					
padlock		padlocks					
payback	ay						
paycheck	ay ch	paychecks					
pickax		pickaxes					
pinprick	pr	pinpricks					
playback	pl ay						
potluck		potlucks					
quicksand	qu nd						

ck

Base	LT's	-s/-es	-ed	-ing	-y/-ly	-er	-est
quickfire	qu ire						
racetrack	ace tr	racetracks					
roadblock	oa bl	roadblocks					
rollback	oll	rollbacks					
rucksack		rucksacks					
sackcloth	cl th						
seasick	ea						
setback		setbacks					
shipwreck	sh wr	shipwrecks					
shockproof	sh pr oo						
sidekick	i-e	sidekicks					
skyjack	y	skyjacks					
smokestack	o-e st sm	smokestacks					
soundtrack	ou nd tr	soundtracks					
starstruck	st ar str						
sunblock	bl						
tailback	ai	tailbacks					
throwback	thr ow	throwbacks					
thumbtack	th mb	thumbtacks					
toothpick	oo th	toothpicks					
truckload	tr oa	truckloads					
wisecrack	i-e cr	wisecracks					
woodblock	oo bl	woodblocks					
yardstick	ar st	yardsticks					

ct

/k-t/ in act

Position: End

Vocalization: Unvoiced

Classification: Blend

Group: End Blends

- **CT** is an end blend. **C** and **T** retain their original sounds.
- End blends are difficult to pronounce in isolation and are therefore best learned through word families: **act, ect, ict, oct, uct**.
- **OCT** is not used in any basic words, but it will be used later in roots like **OCT** in **octopus**.

Base	LT's	-s/-es	-ed	-ing	-y/-ly	-er/-or	-est
act		acts	acted	acting		actor	
duct		ducts					
fact		facts					
pact		pacts					
sect		sects				sector	
strict	str				strictly	stricter	strictest
tact							
tract	tr	tracts				tractor	

Multi-syllable

Base	LT's	-s/-es	-ed	-ing	-y/-ly	-er/-or	-est
abduct		abducts	abducted	abducting		abductor	
addict		addicts	addicted	addicting			
aspect	sp	aspects					

Base	LT's	-s/-es	-ed	-ing	-y/-ly	-er/-or	-est
deduct		deducts	deducted	deducting			
defect		defects	defected	defecting		defector	
detect		detects	detected	detecting		detector	
eject		ejects	ejected	ejecting		ejector	
elect		elects	elected	electing		elector	
enact		enacts	enacted	enacting		enactor	
erect		erects	erected	erecting		erector	
evict		evicts	evicted	evicting			
exact		exacts	exacted	exacting	exactly		

<u>ft</u>

/ft/ in gift

Position: End

Vocalization: Unvoiced

Classification: Blend

Group: End Blends

- **FT** is an end blend. The **F** and **T** retain their original sounds.
- Because end blends are difficult to pronounce in isolation, end blends are best taught through word families: **aft, eft, ift, oft, uft.**

Base	LT's	-s/-es	-ed	-ing	-y/-ly	-er	-est
cleft	cl						
craft	cr	crafts	crafted	crafting	crafty	crafter	
draft	dr	drafts	drafted	drafting	drafty	drafter	
drift	dr	drifts	drifted	drifting	drifty	drifter	
gift		gifts	gifted	gifting			
graft	gr	grafts	grafted	grafting			
heft		hefts	hefted	hefting	hefty	*heftier*	*heftiest*
left		lefts			lefty		
lift		lifts	lifted	lifting		lifter	
loft		lofts	lofted	lofting	lofty	*loftier*	*loftiest*
raft		rafts	rafted	rafting		rafter	
rift							
shaft	sh	shafts	shafted	shafting			
shift	sh	shifts	shifted	shifting	shifty	shifter	
sift		sifts	sifted	sifting		sifter	
soft					softly	softer	softest
swift	sw				swiftly	swifter	swiftest
Taft		Taft's					
thrift	thr				thrifty	*thriftier*	*thriftiest*
tuft		tufts					

Compound

Base	LT's	-s/-es	-ed	-ing	-y/-ly	-er/-or	-est
aircraft	air cr						
airlift	air	airlifts					
chairlift	ch air	chairlifts					
driftwood	dr oo						
facelift	ace ce	facelifts					
gearshift	ear sh	gearshifts					
leftover	er	leftovers					
makeshift	a-e sh						
overdraft	er dr	overdrafts					
shiftless	sh ss						
shoplift	sh	shoplifts	shoplifted	shoplifting		shoplifter	
snowdrift	sn ow dr	snowdrifts					
softball	all						
spacecraft	sp ace cr	spacecrafts					
uplift				uplifting			

ld

/ld/ in held

Position: End

Vocalization: Voiced

Classification: Blend

Group: End Blends

- **-LD** is an end blend
- Long vowel **OLD** and **ILD** words have their own lists in the Closed Syllable Exceptions section. The words in this list are short vowel only.
- **ALD** has its own list in the **AL** section.
- Because end blends are difficult to pronounce in isolation, end blends are best taught through word families. **ELD** is the only short vowel word family for **LD**. The other three, **ALD, ILD,** and **OLD** all have alternative vowel sounds.
- Unlike some of the other end blends, **LD** is combined with the long vowel team **IE (field),** and the **WOR** letter team (**world**). The words **would** and **should** have **LD** endings, but the **L** is silent in those words, so those words belong to the **OULD** team.

Base	LT's	-s/-es	-ed	-ing	-y/-ly	-er	-est
build	ui	builds		building		builder	
field	ie	fields	fielded	fielding		fielder	
held							
shield	ie	shields	shielded	shielding			
weld		welds	welded	welding		welder	
wield	ie	wields	wielded	wielding	wieldy	wielder	
world	wor	worlds			worldly		
yield	ie	yields	yielded	yielding			

See next page for Compound Words

Compound Words

Base	LT's	-s/-es	-ed	-ing	-y/-ly	-er	-est
airfield	air ie	airfields					
battlefield	tle ie	battlefields					
beheld							
coalfield	oa ie	coalfields					
minefield	i-e ie	minefields					
oilfield	oi ie	oilfields					
outfield	ou ie	outfields				outfielder	
upheld							
windshield	nd sh ie	windshields					
withheld	th						

l̲f

/lf/ in shelf

Position: End

Vocalization: Voiced

Classification: Blend

Group: End Blends

- **LF** is an end blend, The **L** and **F** retain their original sounds.
- End blends are best taught through word families: **elf, ilf, olf, ulf**
- **ALF** has its own unique sound. See the **ALF** list for **ALF** words.

Base	LT's	-s/-es	-ed	-ing	-y/-ly	-er	-est
elf		elves					
golf		golfs	golfed	golfing		golfer	
gulf		gulfs	gulfed				
self		selves					
shelf	sh	shelves	shelved	shelving			
wolf		wolves					

Compound

Base	LT's	-s/-es	-ed	-ing	-y/-ly	-er	-est
bookshelf	oo sh	bookshelves					
herself	er						
himself							
itself							
myself	y						
oneself	o-e*						
thyself	th y						
werewolf	o* ere*	werewolves					
yourself	our	yourselves					

160

lk

/lk/ in milk

Position: End

Vocalization: Voiced

Classification: Blend

Group: End Blends

- **LK** is an end blend. End blends are best taught through word families: **elk, ilk, ulk.**
- **ALK** and **OLK** have their own unique sounds. Words ending in **OLK** and **ALK** are listed in the **OLK** and **ALK** lists.

Base	LT's	-s/-es	-ed	-ing	-y/-ly	-er	-est
bilk		bilks	bilked	bilking			
bulk					bulky	bulkier	bulkiest
caulk	au	caulks	caulked	caulking		caulker	
elk		elks					
hulk				hulking			
milk		milks	milked	milking	milky	milkier	milkiest
silk		silks			silky	silkier	silkiest
skulk	sk	skulks	skulked	skulking			
sulk		sulks	sulked	sulking	sulky	sulkier	sulkiest

See next page for **-LK** Compound Words.

Compound

Base	LT's	-s/-es	-ed	-ing	-y/-ly	-er	-est
bulkhead	ea	bulkheads					
milkman							
milkmen							
milkshake	a-e sh	milkshakes					
silkworm	wor	silkworms					
townsfolk	ow olk						

/lp/ in gulp

Position: End

Vocalization: Voiced

Classification: Blend

Group: End Blends

- **LP** is an end blend. The **L** and **P** retain their original sounds.
- End blends are best taught through word families, **alp, elp, ulp**.

Base	LT's	-s/-es	-ed	-ing	-y/-ly	-er	-est
gulp		gulps	gulped	gulping		gulper	
help		helps	helped	helping		helper	
kelp							
pulp							
scalp	sc	scalps	scalped	scalping			
yelp		yelps	yelped	yelping		yelper	

Multi-syllable & Compound

Base	LT's	-s/-es	-ed	-ing	-y/-ly	-er	-est
culpable	ble						
culprit	pr	culprits					
helpful					helpfully		
helpless	ss				helplessly		
palpable	ble						
scalpel	sc	scalpels					
sculpture	ure sc	sculptures					

lt

/lt/ in belt

Position: End

Vocalization: Voiced

Classification: Blend

Group: End Blends

- End blends are best taught through word families: **let, ilt, ult.**
- **ALT** and **OLT** have their own sounds. See the **ALT** and **OLT** lists for words with **ALT** and **OLT** in them.
- **LT** is sometimes combined with **UI (built, guilt).**

Base	LT's	-s/-es	-ed	-ing	-y/-ly	-er	-est
belt		belts	belted	belting			
built	ui*						
cult		cults					
dwelt	dw						
fault	au	faults	faulted	faulting	faulty	*faultier*	*faultiest*
felt							
guilt	ui*				guilty	*guiltier*	*guiltiest*
hilt		hilts					
jilt		jilts	jilted	jilting			
kilt		kilts					
knelt	kn						
lilt		lilts	lilted	lilting			
melt		melts	melted	melting	melty		
pelt		pelts	pelted	pelting			

Base	LT's	-s/-es	-ed	-ing	-y/-ly	-er/-or	-est
quilt	qu	quilts	quilted	quilting		quilter	
shalt	sh						
silt		silts					
stilt	st	stilts	stilted				
tilt		tilts	tilted	tilting			
vault	au	vaults	vaulted	vaulting			
welt		welts					
wilt		wilts	wilted	wilting			

Compound

Base	LT's	-s/-es	-ed	-ing	-y/-ly	-er	-est
beltway	ay	beltways					
sunbelt							

mp

/mp/ in lamp

Position: End

Vocalization: Voiced

Classification: Blend

Group: End Blends

- **MP** is a blend. **M** and **P** retain their original sounds.
- **MP** is an end blend. End blends are best taught through word families: **amp, emp, imp, omp, ump.**

Base	LT's	-s/-es	-ed	-ing	-y/-ly	-er	-est
amp		amps			amply		
blimp	bl	blimps					
bump		bumps	bumped	bumping	bumpy	bumper	
camp		camps	camped	camping		camper	
chimp	ch	chimps					
chomp	ch	chomps	chomped	chomping		chomper	
clamp	cl	clamps	clamped	clamping			
clump	cl	clumps	clumped	clumping	clumpy	*clumpier*	*clumpiest*
cramp	cr	cramps	cramped	cramping	crampy		
crimp	cr	crimps	crimped	crimping		crimper	
damp					damply	damper	dampest
dump		dumps	dumped	dumping	dumpy	dumper	
grump	gr				grumpy	*grumpier*	*grumpiest*
hump		humps					
imp		imps					
jump		jumps	jumped	jumping	jumpy	jumper	
lamp		lamps					
limp					limply	limper	limpest
primp	pr	primps	primped	primping			
pump		pumps	pumped	pumping		pumper	

166

Base	LT's	-s/-es	-ed	-ing	-y/-ly	-er/-or	-est
ramp		ramps	ramped	ramping			
romp		romps	romped	romping		romper	
scamp	sc	scamps				scamper	
skimp	sk	skimps	skimped	skimping	skimpy	*skimpier*	*skimpiest*
slump	sl	slumps	slumped	slumping			
stamp	st	stamps	stamped	stamping		stamper	
stomp	st	stomps	stomped	stomping		stomper	
stump	st	stumps	stumped	stumping		stumper	
sump							
tamp		tamps	tamped	tamping		tamper	
tramp	tr	tramps	tramped	tramping			
tromp	tr	tromps	tromped	tromping			
trump	tr	trumps	trumped	trumping			
wimp		wimps			wimpy	*wimpier*	*wimpiest*

Compound Words

Base	LT's	-s/-es	-ed	-ing	-y/-ly	-er	-est
campfire	ire	campfires					
clampdown	cl ow						
headlamp	ea	headlamps					
humpback	ck						
jumpsuit	ui	jumpsuits					
lamppost	ost	lampposts					
sunlamp		sunlamps					

nd

/nd/ in band

Position: End

Vocalization: Voiced

Classification: Blend

Group: End Blend

- **ND** is an end blend. End blends are best taught through word families: **and, end, ind, ond, und.**
- **IND** has both a short vowel sound **(wind)** and a long vowel sound **(find)**. For words containing long vowel **IND**, see the **IND** list in the Closed Syllable Exceptions section.

Base	LT's	-s/-es	-ed	-ing	-y/-ly	-er	-est
and							
band		bands	banded	banding		bander	
bend		bends	bended	bending	bendy	bender	
bond		bonds	bonded	bonding		bonder	
end		ends	ended	ending		ender	
fend		fends	fended	fending		fender	
fond					fondly	fonder	fondest
found	ou					founder	
friend	ie	friends	friended	friending	friendly	*friendlier*	*friendliest*
fund		funds	funded	funding		funder	
gland	gl	glands					
grand	gr				grandly	grander	grandest
ground	gr ou	grounds	grounded	grounding		grounder	
hand		hands	handed	handing	handy	*handier*	*handiest*
hound	ou	hounds	hounded	hounding			
land		lands	landed	landing			
lend		lends		lending		lender	

Base	LT's	-s/-es	-ed	-ing	-y/-ly	-er/-or	-est
mend		mends	mended	mending		mender	
mound	ou	mounds	mounded	mounding			
pond		ponds					
pound	ou	pounds	pounded	pounding		pounder	
rend		rends		rending		render	
sand		sands	sanded	sanding	sandy	sander	
send		sends		sending		sender	
spend	sp	spends		spending		spender	
stand	st	stands		standing		stander	
tend		tends	tended	tending		tender	
trend	tr	trends	trended	trending	trendy	*trendier*	*trendiest*
wand	wa	wands					
wind ĭ	nd				windy		
wind ī	ind	winds		winding		winder	
wound	ou	wounds	wounded	wounding			

Compound

Base	LT's	-s/-es	-ed	-ing	-y/-ly	-er	-est
backhand	ck	backhands					
bandstand	st	bandstands					
bookend	oo	bookends					
endpoint	oi nt	endpoints					
farmhand	ar	farmhands					
farmland	ar	farmlands					
forehand	ore						
foxhound	ou	foxhounds					
freehand	fr ee						
hairband	air	hairbands					
handbag		handbags					
handball	all						
handbill	ll	handbills					
handbook	oo	handbooks					
handcart	ar	handcarts					
handcuff	ff	handcuffs					
handhold	old	handholds					
handmade	a-e						
handout	ou	handouts					
handover	er						
handrail	ai	handrails					
handsaw	aw	handsaws					

Base	LT's	-s/-es	-ed	-ing	-y/-ly	-er/-or	-est
handset		handsets					
hatband		hatbands					
headwind	ea	headwinds					
homeland	o-e						
inbound	ou						
inland							
landfall	all	landfalls					
landfill	ll	landfills					
landlady	-y	landladies					
landlord	or	landlords					
landmark	ar	landmarks					
landmass	ss	landmasses					
landmine	i-e	landmines					
longhand	ong						
mainland	ai						
neckband	ck	neckbands					
offhand	ff						
outbound	ou						
overhand	er						
parkland	ar	parklands					
sandbag		sandbags					
sandbar	ar	sandbars					
sandbox		sandboxes					
sandman							
sandpit		sandpits					
standby	st y						
standup	st	standups					
tailwind	ai	tailwinds					
upland							
upwind							
weekend	ee	weekends					
wetland		wetlands					
windbag		windbags					
windfall	all	windfalls					
windmill	ll	windmills					
windpipe	i-e	windpipes					
windsock	ck	windsocks					
windsurf	ur	windsurfs					
woodland	oo	woodlands					
woodwind	oo	woodwinds					

<u>nt</u>

/nt/ in ant

Position: End

Vocalization: Voiced

Classification: Blend

Group: End Blend

- **NT** is an end blend. End blends are best taught through word families: **ant, ent, int, ont, unt.**
- The end blend **NT** is added not just to short vowels, but to vowel teams as well, such as **AU, AI, OI,** and **OU.**

Base	LT's	-s/-es	-ed	-ing	-y/-ly	-er	-est
ant		ants					
bent							
blunt	bl	blunts	blunted	blunting	bluntly	blunter	bluntest
bunt		bunts	bunted	bunting		bunter	
burnt	ur						
cent	c(e)	cents				center	
chant	ch	chants	chanted	chanting		chanter	
Clint	cl	Clint's					
count	ou	counts	counted	counting		counter	
dent		dents	dented	denting			
faint	ai	faints	fainted	fainting	faintly	fainter	faintest
flint	fl						
font		fonts					
front	fr	fronts	fronted	fronting			
gent	g(e)	gents			gently		
glint	gl	glints	glinted	glinting			
grant	gr	grants	granted	granting		granter	
grunt	gr	grunts	grunted	grunting		grunter	
haunt	au	haunts	haunted	haunting			
hint		hints	hinted	hinting			
hunt		hunts	hunted	hunting		hunter	
jaunt	au	jaunts	jaunted	jaunting			

171

Base	LT's	-s/-es	-ed	-ing	-y/-ly	-er/-or	-est
joint	oi	joints	jointed				
Lent							
lint							
meant	ea						
mint		mints			minty		
month	o*	months			monthly		
mount	ou	mounts	mounted	mounting	Mounty	mounter	
paint	ai	paints	painted	painting		painter	
pant		pants					
pint		pints					
plant	pl	plants	planted	planting		planter	
point	oi	points	pointed	pointing	pointy	pointer	
print	pr	prints	printed	printing		printer	
punt		punts	punted	punting		punter	
rant		rants	ranted	ranting			
rent		rents	rented	renting		renter	
runt		runts					
saint	ai	saints			saintly		
scant	sc				scanty		
scent	sc c(e)	scents	scented	scenting			
sent							
shunt	sh	shunts	shunted	shunting			
slant	sl	slants	slanted	slanting			
spent	sp						
stunt	st	stunts	stunted	stunting			
taint	ai	taints	tainted	tainting			
tent		tents	tented	tenting			
tint		tints	tinted	tinting			
vent		vents	vented	venting			
want	wa	wants	wanted	wanting			
went	e*						

See next page for **-NT** compound words.

Compound

Base	LT's	-s/-es	-ed	-ing	-y/-ly	-er	-est
anthill	ll	anthills					
basement	a-e	basements					
countless	ou ss				countlessly		
eggplant	gg* pl	eggplants					
indent		indents	indented	indenting			
movement		movements					
pantsuit	ui	pantsuits					
pavement	a-e	pavements					
payment	ay	payments					
suntan		suntans	suntanned	suntanning			
warpaint	ar ai						

pt

/p-t/ in kept

Position: End

Vocalization: Unvoiced

Classification: Blend

Group: End Blends

- **PT** is an end blend. End blends are best taught as word families: **apt, ept, ipt opt, upt.**
- **Upt** is not used in any simple words, but it is used in multi-syllable words as part of the word root, such as *rupt* in *disrupt.*

Base	LT's	-s/-es	-ed	-ing	-y/-ly	-er/-or	-est
apt					aptly		
crept	cr						
crypt	cr y	crypts					
kept							
opt		opts	opted	opting			
rapt						raptor	
script	scr	scripts	scripted	scripting			
slept	sl						
swept	sw						
tempt	mp/pt	tempts	tempted	tempting		tempter	
wept							

Compound

Base	LT's	-s/-es	-ed	-ing	-y/-ly	-er/-or	-est
overslept	er sl						
postscript	ost scr	postscripts					

sk

/sk/ in ask

Position: End (and Beginning)

Vocalization: Unvoiced

Classification: Blend

Group: End Blends

- **SK** is a blend. The **S** and **K** retain their original sounds.
- See **SK** in the beginning blends section for more **SK** words.

End Blend

Base	LT's	-s/-es	-ed	-ing	-y/-ly	-er	-est
ask							
bask		basks	basked	basking			
brisk	br				briskly	brisker	
desk		desks					
disk		disks					
dusk					dusky		
flask	fl	flasks					
husk		husks	husked	husking		husker	
mask		masks	masked	masking			
risk		risks	risked	risking	risky	riskier	riskiest
task		tasks	tasked	tasking			
tusk		tusks					
whisk	wh	whisks	whisked	whisking			

Compound

Base	LT's	-s/-es	-ed	-ing	-y/-ly	-er	-est
desktop		desktops					
taskmaster	st -er	taskmasters					

sp

/sp/ in crisp

Position: End (and Beginning)

Vocalization: Unvoiced

Classification: Blend

Group: End Blends

- **SP** is a blend. The **S** and **P** retain their original sounds.
- **SP** is both a beginning and an end blend. This **SP** list is for end blends. For words that start with **SP**, see the beginning blends section of this book.
- **SP** can be taught in isolation, unlike many other end blends, because it is easier to pronounce than other end blends. The word families for **SP** are **asp**, **isp**, and **usp**.

Base	LT's	-s/-es	-ed	-ing	-y/-ly	-er	-est
clasp	cl	clasps	clasped	clasping			
crisp	cr	crisps	crisped	crisping	crispy/crisply	crisper	crispest
cusp							
gasp		gasps	gasped	gasping			
hasp		hasps					
lisp		lisps	lisped	lisping			
rasp		rasps	rasped	rasping			
wasp	wa	wasps					
wisp	sp	wisps			wispy	wispier	wispiest

No compound words.

st

/st/ in

Position: End and Beginning)

Vocalization: Unvoiced

Classification: Blend

Group: End Blends

- **ST** is a blend. The **S** and **T** retain their original sounds.
- **ST** is both an end blend and a beginning blend. This list is for **ST** as an end blend. For words that start with **ST**, see the beginning blends section of this book.
- **ST** can be taught in isolation, unlike many other end blends, because it is easier to pronounce than other end blends. The word families for **SP** are **ast, est, ist, ost,** and **ust.**
- **ST** in **OST** can be either a short vowel **(cost)** or long vowel **(post)**. See the **OST** list in the closed syllable section for long vowel **OST** words.
- The **ST** end blend is very flexible. **ST** is combined with many different vowel teams and R-controlled syllables, in addition to short vowels.

Base	LT's	-s/-es	-ed	-ing	-y/-ly	-er/-or	-est
angst	ang				angsty		
beast	ea	beasts			beastly		
best		bests	bested				
blast	bl	blasts	blasted	blasting		blaster	
boast	oa	boasts	boasted	boasting		boaster	
boost	oo	boosts	boosted	boosting		booster	
burst	ur	bursts		bursting			
bust		busts	busted	busting		buster	
cast		casts	casted	casting		castor	
chest	ch	chests				Chester	
coast	oa	coasts	coasted	coasting		coaster	
cost		costs		costing	costly	costlier	costliest
crest	cr	crests	crested	cresting			

Base	LT's	-s/-es	-ed	-ing	-y/-ly	-er/-or	-est
crust	cr	crusts	crusted	crusting	crusty	*crustier*	*crustiest*
cyst	c(y)	cysts					
dust		dusts	dusted	dusting	dusty	*dustier*	*dustiest*
east	ea					Easter	
fast		fasts	fasted	fasting		faster	
feast	ea	feasts	feasted	feasting			
first	ir	firsts			firstly		
fist		fists					
foist	oi	foists	foisted	foisting			
frost	fr	frosts	frosted	frosting	frosty	*frostier*	*frostiest*
gist	g(i)						
gust		gusts	gusted	gusting	gusty	*gustier*	*gustiest*
heist	ei	heists					
hoist	oi	hoists	hoisted	hoisting			
jest		jests	jested	jesting		jester	
joist	oi	joists					
joust	ou	jousts	jousted	jousting		jouster	
just					justly		
last		lasts	lasted	lasting	lastly		
least	ea						
lest							
list		lists	listed	listing		lister	
lost							
mast		masts					
midst							
mist		mists	misted	misting	misty	mister	
moist	oi				moistly	moister	moistest
must		musts					
nest		nests	nested	nesting		nester	
past		pasts				pastor	
pest		pests					
quest	qu	quests	quested	questing			
rest		rests	rested	resting			
roast	oa	roasts	roasted	roasting		roaster	
roost	oo	roosts	roosted	roosting		rooster	
roust	ou	rousts	rousted	rousting			
rust		rusts	rusted	rusting	rusty	*rustier*	*rustiest*
test		tests	tested	testing		tester	
toast	oa	toasts	toasted	toasting	toasty	toaster	
trust	tr	trusts	trusted	trusting			
twist	tw	twists	twisted	twisting	twisty	twister	
vast					vastly		

t̲z̲

/ts/ in waltz

Position: End

Vocalization: Unvoiced

Classification: Blend or Digraph

Group: End Blends

- The letter **Z** in **TZ** makes the **/s/** sound. Some educators may consider **TZ** to be a digraph instead of a blend, because the **Z** does not make its traditional **Z** sound. However, since **Z** and **S** often work as alternates, it is listed here in the End Blends section.
- **TZ** words are borrowed words from the German language.
- End blends are best taught as part of word families. The word families for **TZ** are **etz, itz,** and **utz.**

Base	LT's	-s/-es	-ed	-ing	-y/-ly	-er	-est
blitz	bl					blitzer	
chintz	ch						
glitz	gl				glitzy		
hertz	er						
klutz					klutzy	klutzier	klutziest
putz							
quartz	qu ar						
Ritz					ritzy	ritzier	ritziest
spritz	spr	spritzes	spritzed	spritzing		spritzer	
waltz	wa	waltzes	waltzed	waltzing			

Multi-syllable

pretzel	pr	pretzels	
seltzer	er		

Closed Syllable Exceptions

AL words– Printable Cards

all	alm
ald	alt

<u>ald</u>

/ahld/ in bald

Position: End

Vocalization: Voiced

Classification: Closed Syllable Exception

Group: AL-

- **ALD** is one of a group of letter teams that begin with **AL** and have a unique /a/ sound, like the /a/ sound in **ALL**. This group includes **ALL**, **ALM**, **ALT**, and **ALD**.
- There are very few words that contain **ALD**, so some teachers may not teach **ALD** as a separate phoneme.

Base	LT's	-s/-es	-ed	-ing	-y/-ly	-er	-est
bald				balding		balder	baldest
scald	sc	scalds	scalded	scalding			

Multi-Syllable Words

Base	LT's	-s/-es	-ed	-ing	-y/-ly	-er/-or	-est
alderman	-er						
balderdash	-er sh						
caldron		caldrons					
piebald	ie						
ribald							

In some dialects, **ALD** may be pronounced /ld/ in some words, without a clear /a/ sound.

emerald	er	emeralds		
herald	er*	heralds	heralded	heralding

<u>all</u>

/ahl/ or /ol/ in call

Position: End

Vocalization: Voiced

Classification: Closed Syllable Exception

Group: AL-

- **ALL** is pronounced very differently in different parts of the country. In some areas, the **a** sounds similar to the short **/o/** in fog. In other areas, it is pronounced more like **/ah/**.
- **ALL** has two **L's**, but is not part of the **FLOSS** rule. It is a phonogram of its own.
- **ALL** is one of a group of letter teams that begin with **AL** and have a unique **/ol/** sound. This group includes **ALL, ALM, ALT,** and **ALD.**
- **ALL** is specifically an end of a word spelling. When the **/ol/** sound is found at the beginning of a word, it is just spelled **AL,** as in **alto, also, almost,** etc.

Base	LT's	-s/-es	-ed	-ing	-y/-ly	-er	-est
all							
ball		balls	balled	balling			
call		calls	called	calling		caller	
fall		falls		falling			
gall							
hall		halls					
mall		malls					
small	sm					smaller	smallest
stall	st	stalls	stalled	stalling			
tall						taller	tallest
wall		walls	walled	walling			

Compound

Base	LT's	-s/-es	-ed	-ing	-y/-ly	-er	-est
ballgirl	ir	ballgirls					
ballpark	ar	ballparks					
baseball	a-e	baseballs					
downfall	ow	downfalls					
eyeball	eye*	eyeballs					
fallout	all ou						
fastball	st	fastballs					
fireball	i-e	fireballs					
football	oo	footballs					
gumball		gumballs					
hallmark	ar						
hallway	ay	hallways					
handball	nd						
hardball	ll ar						
landfall	nd						
meatball	ea	meatballs					
mothball	th	mothballs					
netball							
outfall	ou						
overall	er						
pinball							
pitfall		pitfalls					
puffball	ff	puffballs					
rainfall	ai						
rockfall	ck	rockfalls					
shortfall	sh or	shortfalls					
smallpox	sm						
snowball	sn ow	snowballs					
softball	ft	softballs					
spitball	sp	spitballs					
stonewall	st o-e						
trackball	tr ck	trackballs					
windfall	nd	windfalls					

alm

/ahlm/ or /olm/ in calm

Position: End

Vocalization: Voiced

Classification: Closed Syllable Exception

Group: AL-

- **ALM** is one of a group of letter teams that begin with **AL** and have a unique /a/ sound, like the /a/ sound in **ALL**. This group includes **ALL**, **ALM**, **ALT**, and **ALD**.

Base	LT's	-s/-es	-ed	-ing	-y/-ly	-er	-est
balm		balms					
calm		calms	calmed	calming		calmer	calmest
psalm	ps	psalms					
qualm	qu	qualms					

Multi-syllable

Base	PG'	-s/-es	-ed	-ing	-y/-ly	-er	-est
almanac		almanacs					
almond	nd	almonds					
almshouse	ou se -s	almshouses					
calmness	ss						
psalmist	ps st						

<u>alt</u>

/ahlt/ or /olt/ in salt

Position: End

Vocalization: Voiced

Classification: Closed Syllable Exception

Group: AL-

- **ALM** is one of a group of letter teams that begin with **AL** and have a unique /a/ sound, like the /**a**/ sound in **ALL**. This group includes **ALL**, **ALM**, **ALT**, and **ALD**.

Base	LT's	-s/-es	-ed	-ing	-y/-ly	-er	-est
halt		halts	halted	halting		halter	
malt			malted				
salt		salts	salted	salting	salty	*saltier*	*saltiest*
schmaltz*	sch						
waltz*		waltzes	waltzed	waltzing			

*Waltz and schmaltz, both ending in **ALTZ**, are words from German origin.

Compound

Base	LT's	-s/-es	-ed	-ing	-y/-ly	-er	-est
saltbox		saltboxes					

Multi-syllable

Base	LT's	-s/-es	-ed	-ing	-y/-ly	-er	-est
alter	er	alters	altered	altering			
asphalt	ph						
basalt							
cobalt							
exalt	ex	exalts	exalted	exalting		exalter	
falter	er	falters	faltered	faltering			
paltry	-y						

NG – Printable Cards

ng	ang
ing	-ing

ong	ung

ang (ng)

/ āng/ in bang

Position: And

Vocalization: Voiced

Classification: Closed Syllable Exception

Group: Ping Pong

- **ANG** belongs to a group of **NG** letter teams, including **ANG, ING, ONG, and UNG**.
- The **NG** end blend is most easily taught as a part of a word family, and not in isolation, due to the difficulty of pronouncing it in isolation.
- Students may need extra practice differentiating between **ANG** and **ANK**, because **ANK** includes the **NG** sound **/angk/**.

Base	LT's	-s/-es/'s	-ed	-ing	-y/-ly	-er	-est
bang		bangs	banged	banging		banger	
Chang	ch	Chang's					
clang	cl	clangs	clanged	clanging			
fang		fangs	fanged				
gang		gangs	ganged	ganging			
hang		hangs		hanging		hanger	
pang		pangs					
rang							
sang							
sprang	spr						
Tang		Tang's					
twang	tw	twangs	twanged	twanging			
Wang		Wang's					
yang							

ang

Compound

Base	LT's	-s/-es	-ed	-ing	-y/-ly	-er	-est
gangway	ay	gangways					
hangman							
hangout	ou	hangouts					

ing (ng)

/ing/ in sing

Position: End

Vocalization: Voiced

Classification: Closed Syllable Exception

Group: Ping Pong

- **ING** belongs to a group of **ng** letter teams, including **ANG, ING, ONG, and UNG**.
- The **NG** end blend is most easily taught as a part of a word family, and not in isolation, due to the difficulty of pronouncing it in isolation.
- Students may need extra practice differentiating between **ING** and **INK**, because the letter team **INK** includes the **NG** sound **/ingk/**.
- **ING** can also be used as a suffix. This list is for words with **ING** as a part of the base word. See the Suffix -**ING** list following this for -**ING** words.

Base	LT's	-s/-es/'s	-ed	-ing	-y/-ly	-er	-est
bring	br	brings		bringing		bringer	
cling	cl	clings		clinging	clingy	*clingier*	*clingiest*
king		kings	kinged	kinging	kingly		
Ling		Ling's					
Ming		Ming's					
ping		pings	pinged	pinging			
ring		rings	ringed	ringing		ringer	
sing		sings		singing		singer	
spring	spr	springs		springing		springer	
swing	sw	swings		swinging			
thing	th	things					
wing		wings	winged	winging			
wring	wr	wrings		wringing		wringer	
zing		zings	zinged	zinging		zinger	

ing

Base	LT's	-s/-es	-ed	-ing	-y/-ly	-er	-est
anything	y th						
clingwrap	cl wr						
downswing	ow sw	downswings					
earring	ear	earrings					
kingpin		kingpins					
kingship	sh						
nothing	th						
offspring	ff spr						
ping-pong							
plaything	pl ay th	playthings					
ringside	i-e						
ringworm	wor						
singsong							
springboard	spr oar	springboards					
springtime	spr i-e						
swingset	sw	swingsets					
upswing	sw						
wellspring	ll spr						
wingspan	sp	wingspans					

suffix -ing

Position: End

Vocalization: Voiced

Classification: Suffix

Group: Suffix

- The number of words that contain the **-ING** suffix is quite large. Each list in this book includes the **-ING** form of each word, so you may consult any list for **-ING** words.
- The previous page has **ING** as a letter team within base words.
- Words that came from Volume 1 base words are starred. *The **VCE** and vowel team patterns are taught in Volume 2, and all of those lists have **-ING** columns.
- The spelling rules for adding **-ING** to one-syllable words are:
  - If a one-syllable word ends in one vowel and one consonant, the consonant is doubled before adding **-ING** (or any vowel suffix). This is called the 1-1-1 rule (one syllable, one vowel, one consonant). The 1-1-1 rule applies to all vowel suffixes, as well. If the word ends in two consonants or has two vowels before the consonant, the last letter is not doubled. The consonant is not doubled when adding consonant suffixes. If a word ends in **W, X**, or **Y**, the last letter is not doubled.
  - If a word ends in an **E**, the **E** is dropped and **-ING** is added.
  - If a single-syllable word ends in any other configuration, (besides **X, E** or 1-1-1), **-ING** is added without any other change.
  - If a word ends in **Y**, generally the **Y** is changed to an **I** before adding a suffix. However, because words of English origin do not have double **i's**, the **Y** is retained when you add **-ING**. This applies to other suffixes that start with **I**, as well.

See next page for -ING list.

-ing

Suffix -ING

Simple	Dropping E	Doubling
taxing *	blaming	batting *
waxing *	blaring	fanning *
fixing *	blinking	mapping *
bleeding	baking	nagging *
blessing *	caring	patting *
blending *	caving	ramming *
blowing	daring	bedding *
clanging *	fading	begging *
clashing *	faking	getting *
cleaning	gaming	letting *
clinging *	glaring	bidding *
fighting	grading	digging *
floating	making	dipping *
banking *	paving	kidding *
clanking *	rating	pinning *
thanking *	shaking	ripping *
blinking *	sharing	sipping *
drinking *	skating	sitting *
shrinking *	stating	tipping *
thinking *	staring	winning *
bonking *	taking	zipping *
honking *	biking	jogging *
dunking *	biting	logging *
binding *	bribing	mopping *
finding *	dining	nodding *
minding *	diving	popping *
blinding *	hiding	potting *
folding *	liking	robbing *
holding *	riding	rotting *
molding *	writing	sobbing *
scolding *	choking	bugging *
rolling *	closing	cutting *
scrolling *	coding	hugging *
strolling *	coping	humming *
bolting *	smoking	lugging *
hosting *	voting	rubbing *
posting *	tuning	running *
chalking *	using	sunning *

<u>ong (ng)</u>

/ong/ in long

Position: End

Vocalization: Voiced

Classification: Closed Syllable Exception

Group: Ping Pong

- **ONG** belongs to a group of **NG** letter teams, including **ANG, ING, ONG, and UNG**.
- The **NG** end blend is most easily taught as a part of a word family, and not in isolation.
- Students may need extra practice differentiating between **ONG** and **ONK**, because **ONK** includes the **NG** sound, **/ongk/**.

Base	LT's	-s/-es	-ed	-ing	-y/-ly	-er	-est
bong		bongs	bonged	bonging			
gong		gongs	gonged	gonging			
long		longs	longed	longing		longer	longest
pong							
prong	pr	prongs	pronged				
song		songs					
strong	str				strongly	stronger	strongest
throng	thr	throngs	thronged	thronging			
tong		tongs					
Wong		Wong's					
wrong	wr	wrongs			wrongly		

See next page for **ONG** compound words.

ong

Compound

Base	LT's	-s/-es	-ed	-ing	-y/-ly	-er	-est
alongside	i-e a-						
birdsong	ir						
daylong	ay						
evensong							
headstrong	ea str						
Hong Kong							
longboat	oa	longboats					
longbow	ow	longbows					
longhand	nd						
longhorn	or	longhorns					
longwise	i-e						
overlong	er						
sidelong	i-e						
singalong	a- ing	singalongs					
singsong	ing						
singsong	ing						
songbird	ir	songbirds					
songbirds	ir						
songbook	oo	songbooks					
songwriter	wr er	songwriters					
strongbox	str	strongboxes					
stronghold	old str	strongholds					
swansong	wa						
wrongdoer	wr -er	wrongdoers					

ung (ng)

/ung/ in lung

Position: End

Vocalization: Voiced

Classification: Closed Syllable Exception

Group: Ping Pong

- **UNG** belongs to a group of **NG** letter teams, including **ANG, ING, ONG, and UNG.**
- The **NG** end blend is most easily taught as a part of a word family, and not in isolation.
- Students may need extra practice differentiating between **UNG** and **UNK,** because **UNK** includes the **NG** sound **/ungk/.**

Base	LT's	-s/-es/'s	-ed	-ing	-y/-ly	-er	-est
bung							
Chung	ch	Chung's					
clung	cl						
dung							
hung							
lung		lungs					
rung							
slung	sl						
sprung	spr						
strung	str						
stung	st						
sung							
swung	sw						
wrung	wr						

NK– Printable Cards

ank

ink

onk

unk

ank (nk)

/ānk/ in bank

Position: End

Vocalization: Voiced

Classification: Closed Syllable Exception

Group: Pink Pig

- **ANK** belongs to a group of **NK** letter teams, including **ANK, INK, ONK, and UNK**.
- The **NK** end blend is most easily taught as a part of a word family, and not in isolation.
- Students may need extra practice differentiating between **ANK** and **ANG**, because **ANK** includes the **NG** sound **/angk/**.

Base	LT's	-s/-es/'s	-ed	-ing	-y/-ly	-er	-est
bank		banks	banked	banking		banker	
blank	bl	blanks	blanked	blanking	blankly		
clank	cl	clanks	clanked	clanking			
crank	cr	cranks	cranked	cranking	cranky	*crankier*	*crankiest*
dank					dankly	danker	dankest
flank	fl	flanks	flanked	flanking			
frank	fr				frankly	franker	frankest
Frank	fr	Frank's					
Hank		Hank's			hanky		
plank	pl	planks	planked	planking			
prank	pr	pranks	pranked	pranking			
rank		ranks	ranked	ranking			
sank							
shrank	shr						
spank	sp	spanks	spanked	spanking			
swank	sw				swanky		
tank		tanks	tanked	tanking		tanker	
thank	th	thanks	thanked	thanking			
yank		yanks	yanked	yanking			

Compound

Base	LT's	-s/-es	-ed	-ing	-y/-ly	-er	-est
banknote	o-e	banknotes					
bankroll	oll	bankrolls					
outflank	ou fl	outflanks	outflanked	outflanking			
outrank	ou	outranks	outranked	outranking			
sandbank	nd	sandbanks					

ink (nk)

/ingk/ in wink

Position: end

Vocalization: Voiced

Classification: Closed Syllable Exception

Group: Pink Pig

- **INK** belongs to a group of **NK** letter teams, including **ANK, INK, ONK, and UNK**.
- The **NK** end blend is most easily taught as a part of a word family, and not in isolation.
- Students may need extra practice differentiating between **ING** and **INK**, because **INK** includes the **NG** sound **/ingk/**.

Base	LT's	-s/-es	-ed	-ing	-y/-ly	-er	-est
blink	bl	blinks	blinked	blinking		blinker	
brink	br					Brinker	
chink	ch	chinks	chinked	chinking			
clink	cl	clinks	clinked	clinking			
drink	dr	drinks		drinking		drinker	
ink		inks	inked	inking	inky		
kink		kinks	kinked	kinking			
link		links	linked	linking			
mink		minks					
pink		pinks	pinked	pinking	pinky	pinker	pinkest
rink		rinks					
shrink	shr	shrinks		shrinking		shrinker	
sink		sinks		sinking		sinker	
slink	sl	slinks		slinking	Slinky		
stink	st	stinks		stinking	stinky	stinker	
think	th	thinks		thinking		thinker	
wink		winks	winked	winking		winker	

ink

Compound

Base	LT's	-s/-es	-ed	-ing	-y/-ly	-er	-est
freethinker	fr ee th -er	freethinkers					
hoodwink	oo	hoodwinks					
hyperlink	y-e er	hyperlinks					
inkstand	st nd	inkstands					
tiddlywink	-ly	tiddlywinks					

onk (nk)

/ongk/ in honk

Position: End

Vocalization: Voiced

Classification: Closed Syllable Exception

Group: Pink Pig

- **ONK** belongs to a group of **NK** letter teams, including **ANK, INK, ONK, and UNK**.
- The **NK** end blend is most easily taught as a part of a word family, and not in isolation.
- Students may need extra practice differentiating between **ONG** and **ONK**, because **ONK** includes the **NG** sound **/ongk/**.

Base	LT's	-s/-es	-ed	-ing	-y/-ly	-er	-est
bonk		bonks	bonked	bonking			
clonk	cl	clonks	clonked	clonking			
conk		conks	conked	conking			
honk		honks	honked	honking			
plonk	pl	plonks	plonked	plonking			
wonk					wonky		
zonk			zonked				

unk (nk)

/ungk/ in honk

Position: End

Vocalization: Voiced

Classification: Closed Syllable Exception

Group: Pink Pig

- **ONK** belongs to a group of **NK** letter teams, including **ANK, INK, ONK, and UNK**.
- The **NK** end blend is most easily taught as a part of a word family, and not in isolation.
- Students may need extra practice differentiating between **UNG** and **UNK**, because the **UNK** letter team includes the **NG** sound **/ungk/**

Base	LT's	-s/-es	-ed	-ing	-y/-ly	-er	-est
bunk		bunks	bunked	bunking		bunker	
chunk	ch	chunks	chunked	chunking	chunky	chunkier	chunkiest
clunk	cl	clunks	clunked	clunking	clunky	clunker	
dunk		dunks	dunked	dunking		dunker	
flunk	fl	flunks	flunked	flunking			
funk					funky	funkier	funkiest
gunk					gunky		
hunk						hunker	
junk					junky	junkier	junkiest
plunk	pl	plunks	plunked	plunking			
punk		punks					
shrunk	shr						
skunk	sk	skunks					
slunk	sl						
spunk	sp				spunky	spunkier	spunkiest
stunk	st						
sunk							
trunk	tr	trunks	trunked				

Kind Old Words
– Printable Cards

ild	ind
old	olt

ost oll

ild

/ī ld/ in wild

Position: End

Vocalization: Voiced

Classification: Closed Syllable Exception

Group: Kind Old Words

- **-ILD** belongs to a group of letter teams that all have a long vowel, even though they are a closed syllable. That team includes **ILD**, **IND**, **OLL**, **OLD**, **OST**, and **OLT**.

Base	LT's	-s/-es	-ed	-ing	-y/-ly	-er	-est
child	ch						
mild					mildly	milder	mildest
wild					wildly	wilder	wildest

Compound

Base	LT's	-s/-es	-ed	-ing	-y/-ly	-er	-est
brainchild	br ai ld						
childbirth	ch ir th						
childcare	ch a-e						
childhood	ch oo						
childless	ch ss						
childlike	ch i-e						
godchild	ch						
grandchild	gr nd ch						
stepchild	st ch						
wildcat		wildcats					
wildfire	i-e	wildfires					
wildlife	i-e						

ind

/ īnd/ in kind

Position: End

Vocalization: Voiced

Classification: Closed Syllable Exception

Group: Kind Old Words

- **IND** belongs to a group of letter teams that all have a long vowel, even though they are a closed syllable. That team includes **ILD, IND, OLL, OLD, OST,** and **OLT.**

Base	LT's	-s/-es	-ed	-ing	-y/-ly	-er	-est
bind		binds		binding		binder	
blind	bl	blinds	blinded	blinding	blindly	blinder	
find		finds		finding		finder	
grind	gr	grinds		grinding		grinder	
hind							
kind					kindly	kinder	kindest
mind		minds	minded	minding		minder	
rind		rinds					

Compound Words

Base	LT's	-s/-es	-ed	-ing	-y/-ly	-er/-or	-est
behind							
blindfold	bl old	blindfolds					
blindside	bl i-e	blindsides	blindsided	blindsiding			
grindstone	gr st o-e	grindstones					
humankind							
mankind							
mastermind	st er	masterminds					
mindset							

<u>old</u>

/ōld/ in gold

Position: End

Vocalization: Voiced

Classification: Closed Syllable Exception

Group: Kind Old Words

- **OLD** belongs to a group of letter teams that all have a long vowel, even though they are a closed syllable. That team includes **ILD, IND, OLL, OLD, OST**, and **OLT**.

Base	LT's	-s/-es	-ed	-ing	-y/-ly	-er	-est
bold					boldly	bolder	boldest
cold		colds			coldly	colder	coldest
fold		folds	folded	folding		folder	
gold							
hold		holds		holding		holder	
mold		molds	molded	molding	moldy	*moldier*	*moldiest*
old						older	oldest
scold	sc	scolds	scolded	scolding		scolder	
sold							
told							

See next page for OLD compound words.

.

old

Compound

Base	LT's	-s/-es	-ed	-ing	-y/-ly	-er	-est
billfold	ll	billfolds					
blindfold	bl ind	blindfolds					
foothold	oo	footholds					
goldmine	i-e	goldmines				goldminer	
goldsmith	sm th	goldsmiths					
handhold	nd	handholds					
holdup		holdups					
household	ou se	households					
toehold	oe	toeholds					
twofold	w*						
undersold	er						
uphold		upholds		upholding		upholder	

oll

/ōl/ in roll

Position: End

Vocalization: Voiced

Classification: Closed Syllable Exception

Group: Kind Old Words

- **OLL** belongs to a group of letter teams that all have a long vowel, even though they are a closed syllable. That team includes **ILD, IND, OLL, OLD, OST,** and **OLT**
- **OLL** has two vowel sounds. One is regular short /ŏ/, and the other is long /ō/. This list is for long **O** only. Short **O OLL** words are in the FLOSS section.

Base	LT's	-s/-es	-ed	-ing	-y/-ly	-er	-est
droll	dr				drolly		
knoll	kn	knolls					
poll		polls	polled	polling			
roll		rolls	rolled	rolling	rolly/roly	roller	
scroll	scr	scrolls	scrolled	scrolling		scroller	
stroll	str	strolls	strolled	strolling		stroller	
toll		tolls	tolled	tolling			
troll	tr	trolls	trolled	trolling		troller	

Compound

Base	LT's	-s/-es	-ed	-ing	-y/-ly	-er/-or	-est
bankroll	ank	bankrolls					
bedroll		bedrolls					
payroll	ay	payrolls					
rollback	ck	rollbacks					
rollover	er	rollovers					
tollbooth	oo th	tollbooths					
tollgate	a-e	tollgates					

<u>olt</u>

/ōlt/ in volt

Position: End

Vocalization: Voiced

Classification: Closed Syllable Exception

Group: Kind Old Words

- **-OLT** belongs to a group of letter teams that all have a long vowel, even though they are a closed syllable. That team includes **ILD, IND, OLL, OLD, OST,** and **OLT.**

Base	LT's	-s/-es	-ed	-ing	-y/-ly	-er	-est
bolt		bolts	bolted	bolting			
colt		colts					
dolt		dolts					
jolt		jolts	jolted	jolting			
molt		molts	molted	molting			
volt		volts					

Compound

Base	LT's	-s/-es	-ed	-ing	-y/-ly	-er	-est
deadbolt	ea	deadbolts					
thunderbolt	th nd -er	thunderbolts					
voltmeter	-er	voltmeters					

ost

/ōst/ in post

Position: End

Vocalization: Voiced

Classification: Closed Syllable Exception

Group: Kind Old Words

- Long **-OST** belongs to a group of letter teams that all have a long vowel, even though they are a closed syllable. That team includes **ILD, IND, OLL, OLD, OST,** and **OLT.**
- **OST** can also be pronounced two ways, short /ŏ/ in frost and long /ō/ in **post** . This list is for long **O**. See the End Blends **ST** section for short **O** **OST** words.

Base	LT's	-s/-es	-ed	-ing	-y/-ly	-er	-est
ghost	gh	ghosts	ghosted	ghosting	ghostly	ghostlier	ghostliest
host		hosts	hosted	hosting		holster	
most					mostly		
post		posts	posted	posting		poster	

See next page for Compound Words

Compound

Base	LT's	-s/-es	-ed	-ing	-y/-ly	-er	-est
bedpost		bedposts					
compost		composts					
doorpost	oor	doorposts					
gatepost	a-e	gateposts					
goalpost	oa	goalposts					
inmost							
outpost	ou	outposts					
postbag		postbags					
postbox		postboxes					
postman							
postmark	ar	postmarks					
signpost	ign	signposts					
topmost							

LK Silent L
– Printable Cards

alk	olk

<u>alk</u>

/ok/ in walk

Position: End

Vocalization: Voiced

Classification: Closed Syllable Exception

Group: Silent Letters (L)

- The **L** in **ALK** is a silent letter, although that may differ, due to dialect.
- The **A** in **ALK** is pronounced **/ah/** or **/o/**, similar to the **AL** letter teams.

Base	LT's	-s/-es	-ed	-ing	-y/-ly	-er	-est
balk		balks	balked	balking			
chalk	ch	chalks	chalked	chalking			
stalk	st	stalks	stalked	stalking		stalker	
talk		talks	talked	talking		talker	
walk		walks	walked	walking		walker	

Compound

Base	LT's	-s/-es	-ed	-ing	-y/-ly
boardwalk	oa	boardwalks			
cakewalk	a-e	cakewalks			
catwalk		catwalks			
chalkboard	ch oa rd	chalkboards			
crosswalk	cr ss	crosswalks			
jaywalk	ay	jaywalks	jaywalked	jaywalking	
sidewalk	i-e	sidewalks			
sleepwalk	sl ee	sleepwalks	sleepwalked	sleepwalking	
spacewalk	sp ace	spacewalks			
walkout	ou				
walkway	ay	walkways			

215

olk

/ōk/ in yolk

Position: End

Vocalization: Voiced

Classification: Closed Syllable Exception

Group: Silent Letters (L)

- The **L** in **OLK** is a silent letter, although that may differ by dialect.
- The **O** in **yolk** is long, similar to the letter teams in Kind Old Words.

Base	LT's	-s/-es	-ed	-ing	-y/-ly	-er	-est
folk		folks			folksy		
yolk		yolks					

Compound

Base	LT's	-s/-es	-ed	-ing	-y/-ly	-er	-est
folklore	ore						
kinfolk							
menfolk							
townsfolk	ow -s						
womenfolk	o*						

Multi-syllable

Base	LT's	-s/-es	-ed	-ing	-y/-ly	-er	-est
polka	a						

Printable Resources

The Resources on the following pages may be copied by one teacher for use in tutoring and classroom settings.

Each blank template is preceded by an example of how to use that template.

Graphics are kept to a minimum on these pages, so that students will not be distracted.

Printable Resources

Page numbers:

Auditory Drill Recording Sheet (Beginner)
Example

b	d	f	h	j	l
a	c	e	g	i	k
m	o	qu	s	u	w
y	n	p	r	t	v
x	z	bl	br	cl	cr
dr	fl	fr	gl	gr	ck
ll	ss	ff			

Auditory Drill

Numbered Auditory Drill

1	2	3	4	5	6
7	8	9	10	11	12
13	14	15	16	17	18
19	20	21	22	23	24
25	26	27	28	29	30
31	32	33	34	35	36
37	38	39	40	41	42
43	44	45	46	47	48
49	50	51	52	53	54

Bingo Board – Example

sh	th	ch	bl	cl
dr	gr	cr	ck	or
ar	er	☆	ir	or
oi	ay	oy	ai	ee
oo	ea	ei	ie	oa

Bingo Board

		★		

Bingo Calling Cards – Example

oo	ea	ei	ie	oa
oi	ay	oy	ai	ee
ar	er	ir	or	dr
gr	cr	ck	or	sh
th	ch	bl	cl	

Bingo Calling Cards

Blending board (3 Elements)
Example

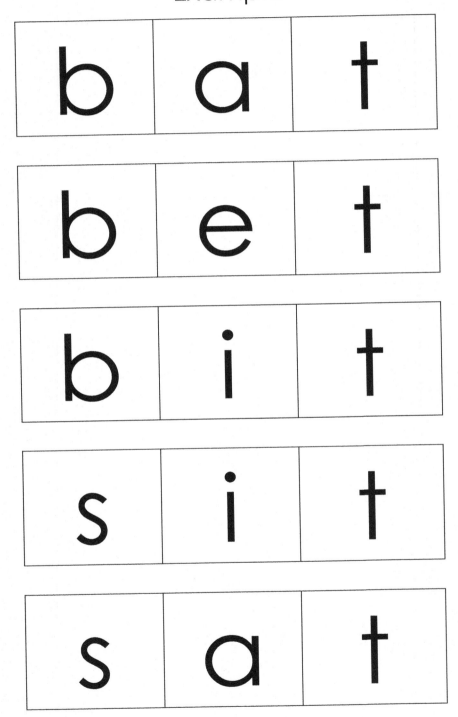

Blending board

Matrix (Beginner) – Example

A matrix maker helps the students to understand the morphemes (meaning elements) of a word. It also helps them to improve their spelling, and to recognize prefixes and suffixes when they are reading. In the example below, the student has just learned -ed, and is reviewing -s and -ing.

Root	Suffix
blast	-s
clean	-ed
	-ing

Words

blasts	cleaned
blasted	cleans
blasting	cleaning

Matrix

Root	Suffix

Words

_____   _____

_____   _____

_____   _____

_____   _____

_____   _____

Phoneme Spelling

3 elements - Example

b	a	t	bat

b	i	t	bit

sh	u	t	shut

ch	a	t	chat

Phoneme Spelling

Phonogram Cards (Blank) – Example

You can use blank phonogram cards to make your own cards that are specific to your student's needs. They can also be used for word practice & to make games.

cei	sing sang song

Phonogram Cards

Phonogram Word Frame

Three Squares - Example

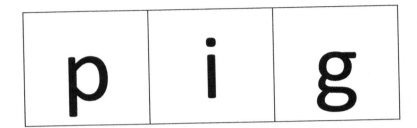

p | i | g

sh | i | p

c | a | t

Word Frame

Reading and Spelling Word List
Large Lined – Example

This paper can be used to make a reading list, or as blank paper for a student's spelling practice. The word list below is an ending CH list.

much _____

ouch _____

beech _____

rich _____

such _____

birch _____

Word List

_____

_____

_____

_____

_____

_____

_____

_____

Sorting Cards (Large) – Example

See the Sorting Frame Example page for sorting ideas.

ship	she
theft	thin
fish	thick
third	shop
shake	shack

Large Sorting Cards

Sorting Frame (2 elements) – Example

Sorting is a very powerful brain-based activity. It is good for both introducing new phonograms, and reviewing old ones. Below is an example of words that have the long /ā/ sound at the end, versus the long /ā/ sound in the middle. **AY** is used for the end, and **AI** is used for the middle.

Students can sort by different concepts, such as sound, letter, beginning/end, voiced/unvoiced. They can also sort by spelling rules. For example, you can do a sort of words that can have a vowel suffix added, and words that need to drop an e before a vowel suffix is added. Students can write the words in the boxes, or you can print out sorting cards (on the following pages), and they can sort using the cards.

If you need to sort four or more concepts, you can use 2 or more frames.

ay	ai
day stay way play	mail fail pail flail

Sorting Frame

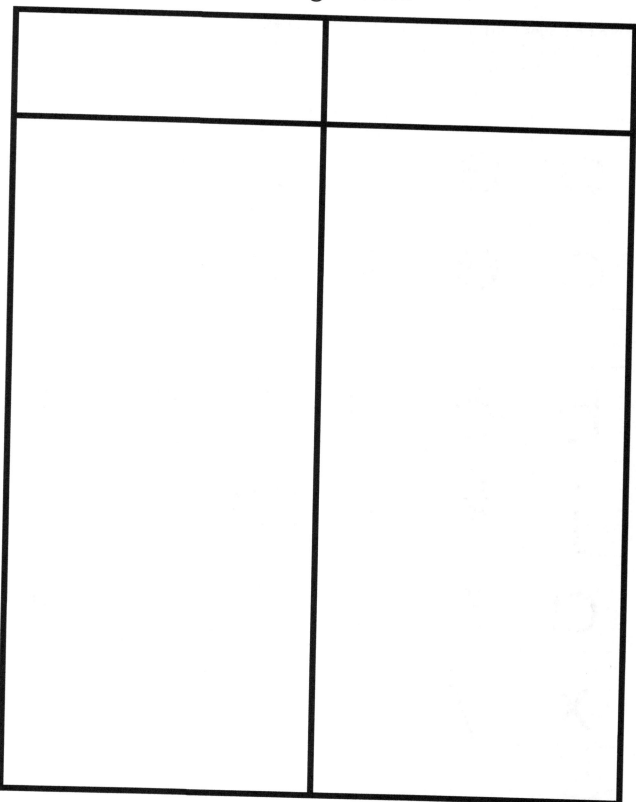

Spelling & Blending Tiles

These tile pages can be photocopied for each child, on tagboard or paper, and then cut apart to make spelling tiles. These tile pages can also be used as a progress chart. Children can color in the box or place a sticker on each phonogram.

a	e	i	o	u	
a	e	i	o	u	

b	c	d	f	g	h
j	k	l	m	n	p
q	r	s	t	v	w
x	y	z			

A	B	C	D	E	F
G	H	I	J	K	L
M	N	O	P	Q	R
S	T	U	V	W	X
Y	Z				

ff	ll	ss	zz		

bl	cl	fl	gl	pl	

sc	sk	sl	sm	sn	sp
st	sw				

br	cr	dr	fr	gr	pr
tr					

dw	tw

ck	ct	ft	ld	lf
lk	lp	lt	mp	nd
nt	pt	sk	sp	st
tz				

all	alt	alm	ald

ang	ing	ong	ung
ank	ink	onk	unk

ild	ind	old	oll
olt	ost		

alk	olk		

Word Segmentation

bed	b	e	d
beg	b	e	g
fed	f	e	d
hem	h	e	m
hen	h	e	n
jet	j	e	t
get	g	e	t
men	m	e	n
pen	p	e	n

Word Segmentation

3 Elements – Example

Word Sums (Beginner)

Example

In the example below, the student is practicing adding -ING, -ED or -S to simple base words.

_bless__ + ___-ing__ = ___blessing_____

___blink___ + ___-s__ = ___blinks_____

___smash___ + ___-ing___ = ___smashing_____

___prick___ + ___-ed___ = ___pricked_____

Word Sums

_____ + _____ = _____

_____ + _____ = _____

_____ + _____ = _____

_____ + _____ = _____

_____ + _____ = _____

_____ + _____ = _____

Printed font differences

(different from handwritten letters)

a	a
g	g

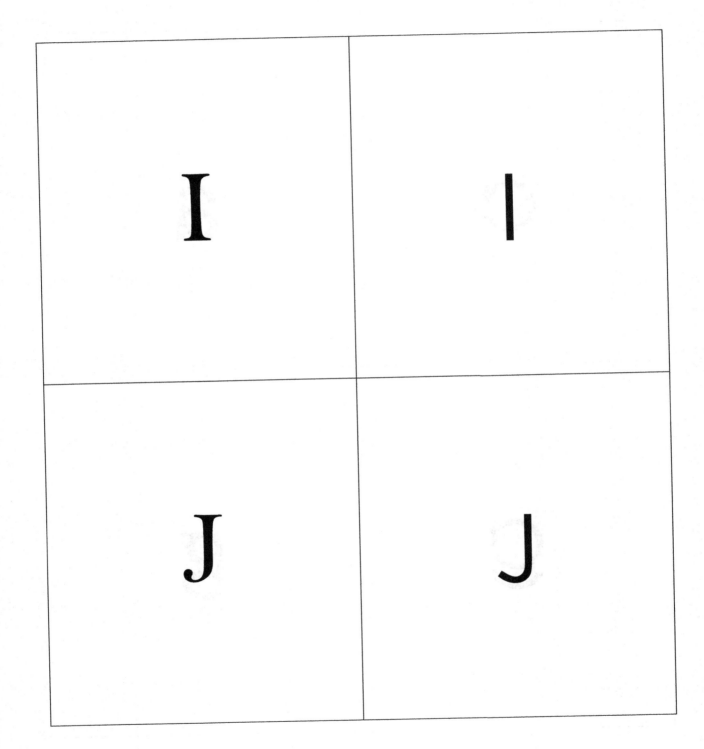

I I

J J

Glossary

Accented Syllable – the syllable that is stressed when the word is pronounced. In the word **ad-VEN-ture**, **VEN** is the accented syllable. In the word **EL-e-phant**, **EL** is the accented syllable. The accent in dictionaries is indicated by an accent mark. **ad ven' ture** **el' e phant** The unaccented syllable often has a schwa sound for the vowel.

Affix – an element that is added to a root or base word to change or modify the meaning of the word. Prefixes and Suffixes are both affixes. In the word, **uncooked, UN-** and **-ED** are both affixes. Affixes are "bound." This means that they cannot stand alone as a word. They must be added to a word to express their meaning.

Base Word – a word that has meaning and can stand on its own. Some people exchange the terms Root Word and Base Word. In this book, a Root Word refers to a word with the smallest unit of meaning. It does not have any prefixes or suffixes. In contrast, in this book, a Base Word is any word that may already have additional prefixes and suffixes added to it. A Base Word that has prefixes or suffixes attached may still be able to have more suffixes and prefixes added to it. For example, in the word **reforming, form** is the **Root** Word. **Reform** could be considered a **Base** Word, because it can stand on its own, and it can have additional suffixes, such as **-ING** added to it **(reforming).** However, **reform** could not be considered a Root Word, because a Root Word would not have a prefix. Roots may or may not be able to stand on their own as words. In the word, **animal, ANIM** is the root, meaning "breath" or "life," but it is not a word on its own.

Blend – two or more letters that appear together frequently, but both retain their original sounds. **PL** is a blend. The **P** and **L** retain their original sounds. **SH** is a digraph, not a blend, because the **S** and **H** in **SH** make a new sound when they are together.

Breve – a marking above a vowel, indicating the vowel's short sound.

ă ĕ ĭ ŏ ŭ

Closed Syllable – syllable that has a single vowel and ends with one or more consonants. In closed syllables, the vowel usually makes a short sound. The word **bet** is a closed syllable, because the consonant **T** "closes" the syllable and causes the **E** to say its short sound. The word **be** is an open syllable. The **E** in **be**

253

says its long sound because there is no consonant closing it. In the word **beside** (be-side), the **be** is an open syllable. In the word **kitten** (kit-ten), **kit** is a closed syllable. In the word **duckling** (duck-ling), **duck** is a closed syllable. Closed syllables can be open at the beginning, as long as they are closed at the end. In the word **advent** (ad-vent), **ad** is a closed syllable.

Closed Syllable Exception – closed syllable with a vowel sound that is not short. In closed syllables, the vowel typically makes a short sound. In closed syllable exceptions, the vowel makes a long sound, or an alternate vowel sound. These are generally taught as their own phonograms. **INK**, **OLD**, and **ALK** are examples of closed syllable exceptions.

Comparative – an adjective or adverb expressing a greater quality. Comparatives end with the suffix **-ER**. **Larger** and **faster** are comparatives. In contrast, Superlatives express the greatest quality and end in **-EST**. **Largest** and **fastest** are superlatives.

Compound Word – A compound word is a word that is made up of at least two smaller words (**baseball, butterfly**). Occasionally, you can have a word that is made up of three or more words, such as **mother-in-law**.

There are three types of compound words:

Closed Compound is a compound word that consists of two or more words that are joined together to make a single word (**playground**). The Closed compound is the most common type of compound word.

Open Compound is a compound that is made up of two words that are separate but function as a single word (**ice cream**).

Hyphenated Compound is a compound word that is made up of two or more words that are joined by a hyphen (**part-time**).

Consonant – A consonant is any letter of the alphabet that is not a vowel. It is a speech sound that is characterized by a closure or obstruction in air/breath. The consonants are **b, c, d, f, g, h, j, k, l, m, n p, q, r, s, t, v, w, x, y,** and **z**. Y is a consonant when it is found at the beginning of a word and makes the sound /y/ in **yam**. Y is vowel when it says /ī/ in **fly**, /ē/ in **bunny**, /ī/ in **type** or /ĭ/ in **gym**.

Consonant Digraph – two consonants that make one consonant sound (**SH, CH**). Blends (**BL, CR**) make two different sounds, but digraphs make only one sound.

Derivational and Inflectional Suffixes – Suffixes are considered either inflectional or derivational. Inflectional Suffixes retain more of the original meaning of the root word than derivations suffixes do. Linguists disagree widely on the differentiation between inflectional and derivational. In general, inflectional suffixes change the verb tense (**-ed, -ing**), indicate number/plural (**-s, -es**), show possession (**'s** in Meghan**'s** bike), and show comparison (**-er, -est**) Derivational suffixes are used to make/derive new words. They change the base word in a more significant way, most often changing the word from one grammar class to another. For example, **kind** (adjective) becomes **kindness** (noun), **hard** (adjective) becomes **harden** (verb).

Digraph – a combination of two letters that represent one sound. **CH** is a consonant digraph and **AI** is a vowel digraph.

Diphthong- a combination of two vowels, in which both vowel sounds are heard, but one vowel sound glides into the other. Those two vowel sounds are found within only one syllable. Experts disagree on the number of diphthongs, but the most common are, **OI, OY, OU,** and **OW.**

End Blend - a blend that appears primarily at the end of a root word. **CT (act), LP (help), NT (ant),** and **SK (brisk)** are all examples of end blends. Suffixes may be added to end blends, so it's important to note that end blends are at the end of root words, not necessarily the end of the word itself: **briskly, helpful, acting.**

Grapheme – the smallest written symbol of a phoneme. The term phoneme refers to the sound, whereas the term grapheme refers to the written letters. A grapheme can be only one letter **(T),** or multiple letters **(OUGH).** The grapheme **SH** symbolizes the phoneme **/sh/** at the beginning of the word **ship.**

Letter Team - any two or more letters that appear frequently together in words. Letter Team is a simplified way to say phonogram, digraph, blend, etc.

Long Vowel – All vowels **(A,E,I,O,U)** have at least two sounds, a short sound, and a long sound. Some vowels have other sounds, as well. The Long Sound is usually identical to the name of the vowel. For example, Long **/ā/** says the name **A,** as in the word **bake.** Long **/ō/** says the name **O,** as in **bone.** Long **U** is the only vowel with two long sounds. The first is pronounced **/yoo/,** like the name of **U,** as in the word **fuse.** The second is **/oo/,** as in the word **tune.** Long vowels are marked by the macron, which looks like a line over the vowel. **ā ē ī ō ū**

Macron - a marking above a vowel, indicating the vowel's long sound.

ā ē ī ō ū

Morpheme – the smallest unit of meaning in a word. Root words can be morphemes, and prefixes and suffixes can also be morphemes. In the word rewrite, **RE** is a morpheme that means "to do again." **WRITE** is a morpheme that means "write." In the word **writer**, **WRITE** is a morpheme that means "write", and ER is a morpheme that means "one who."

Open Syllable – a syllable that ends with a vowel and no consonant. In an open syllable, the vowel usually makes the long vowel sound. In closed syllables, the vowel usually makes a short sound. The word **bet** has a closed syllable, because the consonant **T** "closes" the syllable and causes the **E** to say its short sound. The word **be** is an open syllable. The **E** in **be** says its long sound because there is no consonant closing the syllable. In the word **beside** (be-side), **be** is an open syllable. In the word **kitten** (kit-ten), **kit** is a closed syllable. In the word **duckling** (duck-ling), **duck** is a closed syllable. Closed syllables can be open at the beginning. In the word **advent** (ad-vent), **ad** is still a closed syllable, because it is closed at the end.

Orthographic Mapping – Orthographic mapping is the process of storing printed words into long term memory. It involves seeing a word, breaking the word into letters or letter groups, translating those letters into sounds, and storing the word as a sequence of sounds (and possibly visual images) in the brain. The process or orthographic mapping requires phonemic awareness, understanding of letter/sound relationships and using the phonological long-term memory. Students with dyslexia struggle to map words into long-term memory because of a phonological-core deficit.

Phoneme – A phoneme is the smallest unit of sound in a language. /p/ and /sh/ are both phonemes. The word **boat** has four letters, but it only has three phonemes - /b/, /oa/, /t/.

Phonemic Awareness – awareness of the smallest individual sounds in a word. The terms Phonemic Awareness and Phonological Awareness are often used interchangeably in the field of education. However, phonological awareness is a broader term that refers to a general understanding that words are made up of sounds, whereas phonemic awareness focuses on the individual phonemes (sounds) in a word.

Phonological Awareness – awareness that words are made up of sounds. The terms Phonemic Awareness and Phonological Awareness are often used interchangeably in the field of education. However, phonological awareness is a broader term that refers to a general understanding that words are made up of sounds, whereas phonemic awareness focuses on the individual phonemes (sounds) in a word. Phonological awareness can cover phonemes, but it can also cover syllables, onset & rimes, etc.

Phonogram – A phonogram is a combination of a phoneme (smallest unit of sound) and a grapheme (smallest written unit). Examples of phonograms are **T**, **SH**, **WOR**, and **IGH**.

Prefix – A prefix is added on to the beginning of a base word to change the meaning of that word. Examples of prefixes include **UN-** in the word **unable** and **PRE-** in the word **prewash**.

R-Controlled – An **R**-controlled syllable has a vowel sound that is changed/influenced by the **R**. The **R**-controlled vowels are **AR, ER, IR, OR** and **UR**. Some educators would also include three-letter combinations such as **EAR** and **OAR** to be **R**-controlled.

Root - a word or word part with the smallest unit of meaning. A root word is the most basic form of a word, before prefixes and suffixes are added to it. The terms Root Word and Base Word are frequently used interchangeably in the field of education. In this book, a Base Word may already have a suffix or prefix attached, but the Base Word may still be able to have more suffixes and prefixes added to it, whereas a root word does not have any suffixes or prefixes attached. It is the most basic form of the word. For example, in the word **unzipped**, **zip** is the root word. **Unzip** could be considered a base word, because it can stand on its own, and it can have a suffix (**-ED**) added to it. However, **unzip** could not be considered a root word, because a root word would not have a prefix. Roots may or may not be able to stand on their own as words. In the word, animal, **ANIM** is the root, meaning "breath" or "life," but it is not a root word by itself.

Schwa – a vowel sound that makes an indistinct vowel sound, or no vowel sound at all. The schwa sound is usually found in an unaccented syllable. The sound of the schwa is close to a short /ŭ/ sound, or sometimes a short I /ĭ/ sound, depending on dialect. The schwa sound can be represented by any vowel. The symbol for schwa is "ə" Examples are: **a**bove, pres**e**nt, wiz**a**rd, bott**o**m.

Self-Teaching hypothesis – hypothesis that proposes that children who have proficiency in phonemic awareness and phonic decoding teach themselves to read new words, resulting in a much larger reading vocabulary than could be achieved by learning sight words as whole words. For more information on the Self-Teaching hypothesis, see the research of David Share and Linnea C. Ehri.

Short Vowel – a vowel sound that is cut off, or shortened, by a consonant sound. The short vowels are /ă/ in bat, /ĕ/ in bed, / ĭ / in clip, /ŏ/ in hot, and /ŭ/ in bug.

Silent letter – A silent letter does not have any sound. Silent letters can exist on their own, such as the **H** in the word **herb**, or they can be a part of a letter team, such as the **L** in **OLK** (**yolk**). Silent letters may vary by dialect.

Suffix – an affix that is added on to the end of a root word. Suffixes change the meaning of a word, usually with a change in grammar. For example, in the word **goodness**, the suffix -**NESS** changes the word **good** from an adjective to **goodness**, which is a noun. In **runner**, -**ER** changes the base word from **run**, which is a verb, to **runner**, which is a noun.

Superlative – an adjective or adverb expressing the highest quality. Superlatives end in the suffix -**EST**. **Largest** and **Fastest** are superlatives. In contrast, Comparatives compare and express only a greater quality. Comparatives end in -**ER**. **Larger** and **faster** are comparatives.

Syllable – an uninterrupted unit of speech that has one vowel sound. A syllable can be an entire word, or a part of a word. Examples of words divided into syllables are: **cat, ba-by, ad-vent-ure, cel-e-bra-tion, op-por-tu-ni-ty.** The six syllable types are **Closed, CLE, Open, Vowel Team, VCE,** and **R-Controlled.** Some teachers divide the vowel team syllables into digraphs & dipthongs, making seven syllable types. The word **CLOVER** is a nice way of remembering all of the syllable types. (**C**-closed, **L**-Cle, **O**-open, **V**-vowel team, **E**-VCE, **R**-R controlled)

Trigraph – a combination of a digraph and a third letter **(SHR, CHR).** Trigraphs are sometimes called Digraph Blends.

Unaccented Syllables – all the syllables of a word that are not accented. Vowels in unaccented syllables often express a schwa sound.

Unvoiced (voiceless) - phoneme (speech sound) that uses no vocal cords to produce its sound. All vowels are voiced, so only consonants can be unvoiced. The unvoiced consonant sounds are /**f, h, k, p, s, t, ch, sh**/. **TH** has both a voiced and unvoiced sound. **TH** in **thing** is unvoiced and **TH** in **this** is voiced.

VCE – **VCE** is a syllable pattern. In a **VCE** syllable, the silent **E** at the end of a word causes the preceding vowel to say its long sound. The words **bake, poke,** and meme are all **VCE** words.

Voiced – phoneme (speech sound) that uses vocal cords to produce its sound. All vowels are voiced. The consonant sounds that are voiced are /**b, d, g, j, l, m, n, r, v, w, y, z, ng, zh**/. **TH** has both a voiced and unvoiced sound. **TH** in **thing** is unvoiced and **TH** in **this** is voiced.

Voiceless – See Unvoiced.

Vowel – a sound in which the air is not restricted. The mouth stays open when saying any vowel sound. The vowels are **A,E,I,O,U**, and sometimes **Y.** There are also many vowel teams, such as **AI, EA, OO,** etc.

Vowel Digraph – a combination of two vowels that make one sound. **(AI, EE)**

Vowel Team – a simplified way to say vowel digraph, diphthong, or any other vowel combination.

Bibliography & Resources

for Dyslexia, Phonics, and Word Study

American Heritage Children's Dictionary (2019). Houghton Mifflin Harcourt Publishing Company.

Arredondo, Valerie. (2019). *Orton-Gillingham Word List Dictionary Volume 1, 2 and 3.* Campbell Curriculum.

Ayers, Donald M. (1986). *English Words from Latin and Greek Elements.* University of Arizona Press.

Ayto, John. (2011). *Dictionary of Word Origins.* Arcade Publishing.

Barton Reading & Spelling System. www.bartonreading.com

Bauer, Laurie, et al. (2015). *The Oxford Reference Guide to English Morphology.* Oxford University Press.

Berninger, Virginia. (2016). *Teaching Students with Dyslexia, Dysgraphia, OWL, LD and Dyscalculia.* Paul H. Brookes Publishing Co.

Birsh, Judith. (2011). *Multisensory Teaching of Basic Language Skills.* Paul H. Brookes Publishing Company.

Bishop, Margaret. (1986). *The ABC's and All Their Tricks: The Complete Reference Book of Phonics and Spelling.* Mott Media.

Blevins, Wiley. (2017). *Teaching Phonics & Word Study.* Scholastic.

Carver, Lin & Pantoja, Lauren. (2009). *Teaching Syllable Patterns.* Capstone Publishing, Inc

Dyslexia Training Institute. www.dyslexiatraininginstitute.org

Eide, Brock & Eide, Fernette. (2011). *The Dyslexic Advantage.* Plume.

Eide, Denise. (2012). *Uncovering the Logic of English.* Pedia Learning, Inc.

Fox, Barbara. (2014). *Phonics and Word Study for the Teacher of Reading.* Pearson.

Freeman, David & Freeman, Yvonne. *Essential Linguistics.* Heinemann.

Fulford, John. (2012). *The Complete Guide to English Spelling Rules.* Astoria Press.

Galaburda, Albert, et al. (2018). *Dyslexia and Neuroscience.* Paul H. Brookes Publishing Co.

Ganske, Kathy, (2014). *Word Journeys.* Guilford Press.

Ganske, Kathy. (2008). *Mindful of Words*. Guilford Press.

Geffner, Donna. (2019). *Auditory Processing Disorders: Assessment, Management, and Treatment*. Plural Publishing.

Gillingham, Anna & Stillman, Bessie. *The Gillingham Manual*. Educators Publishing Service.

Haspelmath, Martin and Sims, Andrea. (2002). *Understanding Morphology (Understanding Language Series)*. Routledge.

Henry, Marcia. (2010). *Unlocking Literacy: Effective Decoding & Spelling Instruction*. Paul H. Brookes Publishing Co.

Henry, Marcia. (2010). Words: *Integrated Decoding and Spelling Instruction Based on Word Origin and Word Structure*. Pro-Ed.

Institute for Multi-Sensory Education. www.orton-gillingham.com

International Dyslexia Association. www.dyslexiaida.org

Johnson, Kristin and Bayrd, Polly. (2010). *Megawords (series)*. Educators Publishing Service.

Honig, Bill & Diamond, Linda. (2019). *Teaching Reading Sourcebook (Core Literacy Library)*. Academic Therapy Publications; Third edition.

Kilpatrick, David, et al. (2019). *Reading Development and Difficulties: Bridging the Gap Between Research and Practice*.

Kilpatrick, David. (2016). *Equipped for Reading Success*. Casey & Kirsch Publishers.

Kilpatrick, David. (2015). *Essentials of Assessing, Preventing, and Overcoming Reading Difficulties*. John Wiley & Sons, Inc.

Leu, Donald & Kinzer, Charles. (2017). *Phonics, Phonemic Awareness, and Word Analysis*. Pearson Education, Inc.

Lewis, Norman. (2014). *Word Power Made Easy*. Anchor Press.

Mather, Nancy. (2009). *Writing Assessment and Instruction for Students with Learning Disabilities*. Jossey-Bass (Wiley).

Minkova, Donka (2004). "Philology, linguistics, and the history of /hw/~/w/". In Anne Curzan; Kimberly Emmons (eds.). *Studies in the History of the English language II: Unfolding Conversations*.

Mather, Nancy. (2012). *Essentials of Dyslexia Assessment and Intervention*. John Wiley & Sons, Inc.

Moats, Louisa Cook. (2010). *Speech to Print: Language Essentials for Teachers*. Paul H. Brookes Publishing Co.

Moats, Louisa & Toman, Carol. *LETRS* training program for teachers.

Neil Ramsden Word Searcher. www.neilramsden.co.uk

O'Connor, Rollanda E. (2020). *Teaching Word Recognition.* The Guildord Press.

Online Etymology Dictionary. www.etymonline.com

Orton Gillingham Online Academy. www.ortongillinghamonlinetutor.com

Reid, Gavin & Guise, Jennie. (2017). *The Dyslexia Assessment.* Bloomsbury.

Rippel, Marie. All About Learning curriculum. www.allaboutlearningpress.com

Rome, Paula & Osman, Jean. (2000). *Advanced Language Tool Kit.* Educators Publishing Services.

Rome, Paula & Osman, Jean. (2004). *Language Tool Kit.* Educators Publishing Services.

Ruding, Joanne. (2017). *Spelling Rules Workbook.* How to Spell Publishing.

Shaywitz, Sally. (2003). *Overcoming Dyslexia.* Vintage Books.

The Yale Center for Dyslexia & Creativity. www.dyslexia.yale.edu

Venezky, Richard. (1999). *The American Way of Spelling: The Structure and Origins of American English Orthography.* Guilford Press.

Wilson Reading System. www.wilsonlanguage.com

Zafarris, Jess. (2020). *Once Upon a Word: A Word-Origin Dictionary.* Rockridge Press.

Made in the USA
Middletown, DE
02 September 2023

37827093R00150